Modern Diesel Power

by Brian Solomon

Voyageur Press

First published in 2011 by Voyageur Press, an imprint of MBI Publishing Company, 400 First Avenue North, Suite 300, Minneapolis, MN 55401 USA

The information in this book is true and complete to the best of our knowledge. All recommendations are made without any guarantee on the part of the author or Publisher, who also disclaims any liability incurred in connection with the use of this data or specific details.

We recognize, further, that some words, model names, and designations mentioned herein are the property of the trademark holder. We use them for identification purposes only. This is not an official publication.

Voyageur Press titles are also available at discounts in bulk quantity for industrial or sales-promotional use. For details write to Special Sales Manager at MBI Publishing Company, 400 First Avenue North, Suite 300, Minneapolis, MN 55401 USA.

To find out more about our books, visit us online at www.voyageurpress.com.

ISBN: 978-0-7603-3943-5

Solomon, Brian, 1966–
  Modern diesel power / Brian Solomon.
      p. cm.
  Includes bibliographical references and index.
  ISBN 978-0-7603-3943-5 (pbk.: alk. paper)
  1. Diesel locomotives—United States. 2. Electro-diesel locomotives—United States. 3. General Electric Company. I. Title.
   TJ619.2.S65285 2011
   625.26′620973022—dc22
                          2010036611

Cover: After loading taconite pellets under northern Minnesota's bright early-autumn skies, BNSF No. 5973 departs U.S. Steel's Minntac plant in Mt. Iron, beginning the all-rail trip south to the steelmaker's Fairfield facility near Birmingham, Alabama. BNSF played a key role in the development of the GE Evolution series and eventually ordered some 600 ES44ACs for heavy freight service. © *Todd Mavec*

Frontispiece: On December 1, 2004, a Metra MP36PH-3S leads a commuter train at Grayslake, Illinois. The MPXpress, in its many variants, has become the most common new power for commuter services in North America. *Chris Guss*

Title pages: As of mid-2010, Toronto-based GO Transit had the only fleet of Motive Power–built MP40PH-3Cs. These 4,000-horsepower locomotives are significantly more powerful than the 1980s-era F59PHs they supplanted. Here, GO No. 601 races east of Toronto Union Station at Bathurst Street on June 11, 2010. *Brian Solomon*

Editor: Dennis Pernu
Design Manager: Brenda C. Canales
Designer: Chris Fayers

Printed in China

Contents

Acknowledgments

In the last 25 years, I've had the fortune to spend considerable time trackside, studying and photographing modern locomotives at work. I could not have done this without the assistance of many people. Along the way I've traveled with many photographers and met with railroaders and locomotive industry professionals who have imparted valuable information. My understanding of modern diesels, the details of their operation, and where they are assigned represents a collective body of knowledge accumulated over the years through careful study of written materials, close observation of locomotives in operation, visits to locomotive shops, detailed discussions with experts, and a continuous exchange of emails.

Thanks to: Mike Abalos, Howard Ande, Marshall Beecher, R. T. Berryman, Jim Boyd, Phil Brahms, Robert A. Buck, Brian Burns, Greg Cruickshank, Mike Danneman, Tom Danneman, Tim Doherty, Doug Eisele, Mike Gardner, Phil Gosney, Don Gulbrandsen, Sean Graham-White, John Gruber, Chris Guss, Brad Hellman, Mark Hemphill, Don Jilson, Bill Keay, Tom Kline, George W. Kowanski, Tom M. Hoover, T. S. Hoover, Brian L. Jennison, Don Marson, Mel Patrick, George S. Pitarys, Brian Plant, Doug Riddell, Pete Ruesch, Brian Rutherford, J.D. Schmid, Scott Snell, Joe Snopek, Chris Southwell, Dave Stanley, Vic Stone, Dave Swirk, Mike Valentine, Otto Vondrak, Craig Willette, and Patrick Yough.

Special thanks to Norfolk Southern's Don Graab for details regarding NS's SD40E locomotives.

Among the wealth of written material I've consulted were informative and entertaining articles by Sean Graham-White, David Lustig, Greg McDonnell, Jay Potter, Dale Sanders, Paul Schneider, and David C. Warner, and books by John F. Kirkland, Louis A. Marre and Jerry A. Pinkepank, and Paul Withers. Past issues of locomotive magazines *Extra 2200 South* and *Diesel Era* were invaluable resources for establishing specifics regarding American diesel production. Reviewing past issues of *Railway Mechanical Engineer* and *Railway Age* provided a level of detail rarely found today in railway trade publications and offered a degree of inspiration. Locomotive manufacturers Brookville Equipment

Since 1999, Alaska Railroad has assembled a small fleet of SD70MACs, buying them new from Electro-Motive in small batches. Significantly, it is the only railroad to routinely assign SD70MACs in passenger service. *Scott R. Snell*

Corporation, Electro-Motive Diesel, General Electric, MotivePower, and R. J. Corman Railpower provided very informative websites with detailed and up-to-date information.

Although I made many of the images in these pages, a great number were contributed by my fellow photographers, each of whom is appropriately credited beside their images.

My father, Richard Jay Solomon, provided editorial and tech support, and my mother, Maureen Solomon, assisted with travel logistics and office support.

Thanks to my editor, Dennis Pernu, and everyone at Voyageur Press for making my concept into the volume you hold in your hands.

Introduction

Introduction

First, some terminology. When we speak of a modern *locomotive*, we refer to the entire machine. North American diesel-electric locomotives are powered by a diesel engine that is coupled to a generator/alternator, which in turn powers electric traction motors that turn the locomotive's powered axles. Although *engine* is often used to describe the entire locomotive, in this book it refers specifically to the prime mover (i.e., the diesel engine) inside the locomotive. Since two or more diesel locomotives are routinely used to haul trains, individual locomotives are referred to as *units*.

During the 1960s, a power race between North American locomotive manufacturers resulted in the doubling of horsepower offered by typical one-engine, single-unit diesel-electric locomotives, while massive "double diesels" pushed the single unit to more than 6,000 horsepower (although only Union Pacific and Southern Pacific availed themselves of these monsters). In the 1970s, locomotive builders focused on refining designs to improve reliability rather than boosting output. During the 1980s,

demands for improved fuel economy and greater reliability were met through advances in microprocessor technology, while onboard computers and advanced wheel-slip control improved performance through tighter management of locomotive systems.

In the late 1980s and 1990s, trends toward improved crew safety resulted in the wide-scale adoption of the North American Safety Cab on locomotives built for service in the United States, thus greatly changing the outward appearance of locomotives. In the late 1980s and early 1990s, single-engine output was pushed to 4,400 horsepower using existing technologies. During this phase of development, improvements to electrical systems, combined with efforts to speed the manufacturing process (and a desire by some railroads to employ fewer locomotive types), effectively eliminated the cost advantages once offered by four-motor freight types versus six-motor types. The last new high-horsepower, four-motor road-freight diesels were built in 1994. Since then, virtually all new road-freight diesels have had six axles.

The most important innovation of the early 1990s was the practical development

An EMD-built DM30AC belonging to Long Island Rail Road hums on the platform at Jamaica, New York, in March 2003. *Brian Solomon*

of three-phase alternating current traction systems by both Electro-Motive and General Electric. The technological advances necessary to make them practical in the rigorous North American locomotive environment required intensive investment of time, skills, and resources. Both manufacturers needed substantial interest from railroads to ensure they would recoup their investment.

Three-phase AC motors are virtually free from limitations associated with DC motors when operating at maximum load (DC motors are limited by short time ratings to keep them from overheating). Additionally, three-phase AC motors offer superior wheel-slip control and extended-range dynamic braking, both of which greatly aid operation of heavy trains in graded territory while reducing costs. Because AC locomotives offer the ability to operate at maximum load at virtually any speed with minimal risk of motor damage or stalling, they were viewed as ideal for movement of heavy unit coal trains. Railroads seeking to reduce operating costs for this valuable traffic were willing to take the risk and placed significant orders for AC traction, thus allowing for its refinement.

Where EMD initially worked with Burlington Northern, GE partnered with CSX. Each manufacturer went about AC traction a different way. EMD teamed with

Previous pages:
Iowa Interstate General Electric ES44ACs wait with a freight at Blue Island, Illinois, as a Chicago Metra MP36PH-3S shoves east with a commuter train. High-horsepower freight units and specially designed passenger models are the two most common varieties of modern diesel-electric locomotives working North American railroads. *Marshall W. Beecher*

the German firm Siemens in the adaptation of European technology to American operating conditions, while General Electric refined the technology independently. The primary electrical difference between EMD's and GE's AC-traction systems is in the arrangements of the inverters—banks of high-tech electrical equipment that convert direct current to a form of modulated, three-phase alternating current for traction. The EMD-Siemens AC control system uses two inverters, one for each truck (one inverter controls three motors); General Electric uses six inverters per locomotive, which permits individual axle control and thus enables higher tractive effort while affording greater reliability.

In the mid-1990s, both manufacturers built both AC- and DC-traction locomotives in the 4,000- to 4,400-horsepower range while simultaneously advancing technology for the production of 6,000-horsepower single-engine diesels. To achieve this, both EMD and GE developed new diesel engines capable of much greater output. The theory behind a single 6,000-horsepower locomotive was based on unit reduction and component reduction. As the fleets of 1960s- and 1970s-era 3,000-horsepower diesels approached retirement age, it was expected that railroads could replace two retired locomotives with one. While both manufacturers produced commercial 6,000-horsepower locomotives, the anticipated market for these types didn't develop and relatively few were sold.

In the last decade, locomotive development has been driven largely by more stringent air-quality standards. Manufacturers have faced the challenge of reducing the volume of pollutants emitted by diesel engines while maintaining high fuel economy without sacrificing output or reliability. Because one method of reducing emissions is through improved cooling, the most modern diesel-electrics are typified by their enormous radiators at the back of the locomotive body. Other design influences affecting new locomotive types are crash-worthiness standards intended to better protect crews and prevent fuel leakage in the event of collisions, and the need to equip locomotives with modern signaling equipment necessary for positive train control.

During the last decade, passenger locomotives, once the domain of the large builders, have been built largely by smaller manufacturers. Likewise, lower horsepower diesels used for switching have been built by a variety of smaller companies.

This book focuses on successful new locomotive designs introduced since 1980, with an emphasis on types built since the advent of microprocessor controls. Although a great variety of models in operation on North American railroads are depicted, this book is not intended as a comprehensive identification guide.

Opposite: State-of-the-art in the mid-1980s, older General Electric Dash 8s are now considered "classics." On May 12, 2007, Norfolk Southern C39-8 No. 8554 leads a westward freight across the former Erie Railroad trestle at Portage, New York. *Brian Solomon*

Chapter 1

General Electric

General Electric

I n the 1980s, General Electric emerged as America's foremost diesel builder. Key to its commercial advantage were diesel-electric technologies that enabled GE to deliver substantially more reliable locomotives, known as its new Dash 8 line.

In the 1980s, computer technology had matured to the point where it could withstand the rigors of a locomotive operating environment, while being small enough for convenient placement within the confines of a modern locomotive. The Dash 8 design used three computers: one to oversee locomotive control functions, one to manage the main alternator, and one to control the fans and blower motors. The computers run programs that optimize performance for respective components while protecting key systems from overuse. Diagnostic features track and record component performance while monitoring external conditions.

Among other Dash 8 advances was a new traction alternator/rectifier design with power enough to supply both sufficient current for starting and sufficient voltage for high speeds without the need for electrical transition stages that matched alternator output with motor requirements.

The Dash 8 era began with experimental prototypes: a 3,600-horsepower four-axle designated B36-8 and a six-motor machine designated C39-8. Like other modern GE high-horsepower diesels, these were powered by the company's proven 16-cylinder FDL engine and the latest GE 752 traction motor. Rather than immediately supplant its proven Dash 7 line, GE strengthened its new technology by introducing a few small fleets of preproduction Dash 8 locomotives to be used by railroads in regular revenue service while serving as test beds for further development and encouraging railroad interest in the new product line. GE began mass production of the Dash 8 line in 1987, initially offering two models: the four-motor Dash 8-40B and the six-motor Dash 8-40C.

In 1989, the North American Safety Cab made its commercial debut. The transition to safety cab designs coincided with Dash 8 production. Mass-produced Dash 8-40CWs (*W* referring to the safety cab design that features a wider nose section) were first sold to Union Pacific in 1990. Within a few years most of GE's customers were purchasing locomotives with North American Safety Cabs, and only a few lines, such as Norfolk

Southern, continued to order the traditional cab design.

General Electric introduced its Dash 9 line in 1993. Compared with the Dash 8, which had implemented a variety of significant design changes, the Dash 9 was more of a marketing tool to distinguish smaller improvements that resulted in more capable locomotives and lower lifecycle costs. Innovations like electronic fuel injection and split cooling were first offered as options on late-era Dash 8s, but became standard features with the Dash 9 and would help GE meet more stringent air-quality requirements in the decade following the Dash 9's introduction. Other Dash 9 features included the high-adhesion HiAd truck and nominal external changes, such as a more ergonomic step and handrail arrangement to improve crew safety and comfort.

Far more significant than the Dash 9 was GE's first commercial alternating current traction locomotive. While both the DC-traction Dash 9 and the AC-traction AC4400CW are rated at 4,400 horsepower, AC traction was a major technological leap. Computer-controlled three-phase AC power substantially increased the tractive effort of an individual locomotive (allowing it to haul more tonnage) and improved dynamic braking capability while lowering electrical lifecycle costs.

Among the variations of this revolutionary locomotive were CSX's 500 series AC4400CWs, which are unusual in CSX's GE fleet because they carry an extra 10 tons of ballast to boost their tractive effort in slow-speed mineral service on very steep grades. In addition, CSX, Kansas City Southern, and CP Rail bought AC4400CWs with steerable GE trucks designed to reduce wheel and rail wear.

In the mid-1990s, GE introduced the AC6000CW as a high-horsepower competitor for EMD's SD90MAC-H, developed about the same time. Interest in this high-horsepower model stemmed in part from the cost advantages associated with unit reduction—one 6,000-horsepower diesel could replace a pair of 1970s-era EMD SD40-2s or GE C30-7s. To achieve this extreme horsepower, GE teamed with German engine manufacturer Deutz MWM in development of the 16-7HDL. This engine, like the long-established 16-7FDL, is a four-cycle design employing 16 cylinders in a 45-degree V configuration.

Among the striking features of the AC6000CW is a larger carbody and radiators with massive "wings" at the rear of the locomotive. Some AC6000CWs were "convertibles" built with the 4,400-horsepower 7FDL diesel, capable of a later upgrade to the more powerful engine. Only Union Pacific and CSX bought the AC6000CW, and the 6,000-horsepower concept fell out of favor before the model was built in large numbers. As a result, these big diesels remain among the more uncommon modern types.

Introduction of the Environmental Protection Agency's more stringent engine emissions requirements has played a significant role in recent GE locomotives. While GE was able to adapt its 7FDL engine to meet EPA Tier 0 and Tier 1 requirements, in order to comply with Tier 2 requirements that went into effect in 2005, GE engineered a new diesel engine, known as the GEVO, an evolutionary advancement of the FDL design. The GEVO was integral to introduction of GE's Evolution series, which can be ordered with either DC or AC traction, depending on intended application. As with the Dash 8s in the mid-1980s, in 2003 and 2004 GE built 50 preproduction locomotives for UP, BNSF, and NS, enabling GE to gain field experience with new configurations *before* it was required to meet Tier 2 standards in regular production.

Because few design changes were required, the preproduction units share a similar appearance with production Evolution units. The ES44AC and ES44DC remain GE's standard production models. A recent variation is the ES44C4, an AC-traction model that employs A1A trucks, allowing for a six-axle, four-motor model. This offers performance characteristics similar to DC traction Evolution locomotives, but provides some of the operating cost advantages of AC traction without the high price tag of a six-motor AC-traction model. In the future, the ES44C4 and similar models may result in the phasing out of GE's DC-traction line.

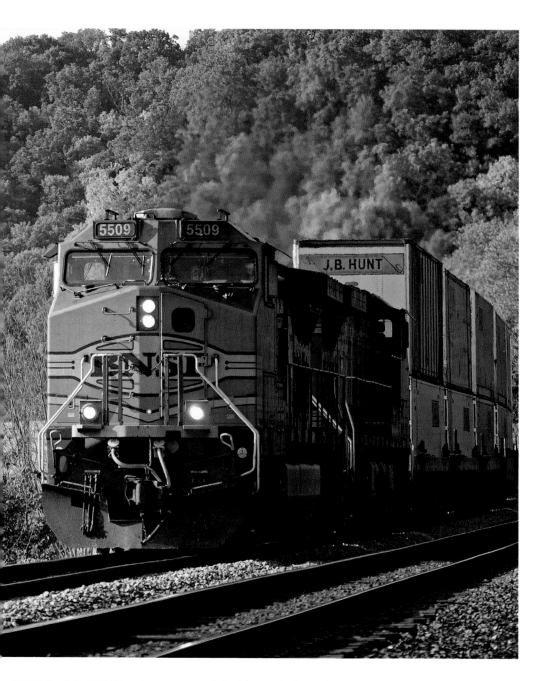

BNSF Dash 9-44CW leads an eastward double-stack along the Mississippi at Savanna, Illinois, on June 24, 2010. The Dash 9 employed variations of the 16-7FDL diesel and GE 752 traction motor, and it represents 30 years of engineering refinement. *Brian Solomon*

On July 8, 1994, leased LMX B39-8s bracket a cabless Burlington Northern B30-7A and lead an eastward intermodal train on the former Great Northern at Grizzly, Montana. The fleet of GE's LMX subsidiary represented the manufacturer's first full-service maintenance contract. GE serviced the locomotives at the old Chicago, Burlington & Quincy shops in Lincoln, Nebraska. *Brian Solomon*

An LMX B39-8 leads an eastward BN intermodal train on the Aurora Sub at Oregon, Illinois, on February 19, 1995. Except for three B32-8 preproduction prototypes, BN didn't operate Dash 8s dressed in its famous Cascade Green livery. *Brian Solomon*

New Conrail Dash 8-40B No. 5066 leads Chicago–Boston intermodal train TV14 at East Rochester, New York, on May 4, 1988. To convey the new line's higher quality, GE incorporated "Dash" into its new designations. While a clever marketing ploy, many railroads perpetuated the old classification system, which has resulted in confusion. *Brian Solomon*

In July 1989, Conrail B40-8 No. 5079 leads a westward intermodal upgrade on the old Pennsylvania Railroad at MG Tower. Conrail painted its Dash 8-40B fleet with a nose logo meant to represent new era of cooperation between labor and management. *Brian Solomon*

In 1988, short-line operator New York, Susquehanna & Western bought four Dash 8-40Bs—built to Conrail specifications—for service on high-priority intermodal trains. In spring 1989, after NYS&W was designated operator of the bankrupt Delaware & Hudson, the railroad placed a second order that was backed by CSX. After D&H operations were conveyed to CP Rail in 1990, CSX took title of the second order. New B40-8 No. 4034 was seen at SK Yard in Buffalo, New York, on May 4, 1989. *Brian Solomon*

A warm morning on July 6, 1987, finds Conrail C32-8 No. 6613 and a pair of C30-7As leading eastward freight on the old Boston & Albany main line below the Massachusetts Turnpike at Woronoco. *Brian Solomon*

Norfolk Southern C39-8 No. 8669 leads a short Hanjin double-stack at Tifft Street in Buffalo, New York, in July 1989. When new, these NS locomotives were set up to run long hood forward. *Brian Solomon*

During Dash 8 development, GE built four fleets of prototypes for extensive road-service testing. Conrail tested 10 C32-8s (Nos. 6610–6619), unusual 3,250-horsepower six-motor models powered by the 12-cylinder FDL engine. On June 10, 1987, Conrail No. 6617 leads westward freight MBSE (Middleborough, Massachusetts, to Selkirk, New York) at West Brimfield, Massachusetts. *Brian Solomon*

General Electric's Dash 8-40C was a six-motor production model rated at 4,000 horsepower. Chicago & North Western No. 8548, with a westward, waits for a meet on April 22, 1995, just a few days before C&NW was officially absorbed into the Union Pacific system. *Brian Solomon*

Above: The Dash 8-40C was one of GE's biggest successes of the mid-1980s, reestablishing its reputation with railroads that had largely purchased EMD locomotives in the 1960s and 1970s and filling large orders with stalwart customers, such as CSX. On October 16, 2004, CSX Dash 8-40C No. 7530 and a former Conrail SD60 lead an eastward freight on the old West Shore Route at Guilderland, New York. *Brian Solomon*

Opposite: Conrail No. 6031 leads an excursion at Exchange Street in Buffalo, New York, on July 2, 1989. Difficulties with preserved Nickel Plate Road 2-8-4 No. 765 resulted in this rare use of a Dash 8-40C in passenger service. *Brian Solomon*

Above: Union Pacific Dash 8-40C No. 9335 works westward through Nevada's Clover Creek Canyon on March 3, 1997. Among the Dash 8 line's many advances was a powerful traction alternator/rectifier capable of supplying high voltage and high current to motors, and thus avoiding the need for complex motor transition circuitry that had been common on earlier models. *Brian Solomon*

Opposite top: A pair of Union Pacific Dash 8-40Cs leads an eastward grain train at Chappell, Nebraska, on September 26, 1989. *Brian Solomon*

Opposite bottom: Union Pacific Dash 8-40C No. 9184 races along in eastern Wyoming on September 26, 1989. The Dash 8 design used refined versions of GE's primary components: the successful FDL diesel engine and 752 series traction motors. Introduced with the Dash 8, the 752AG motor enabled GE to boost continuous tractive effort ratings by 5 to 11 percent over previous models. *Brian Solomon*

Former Santa Fe Dash 8-40BWs lead an eastward BNSF carload freight in eastern Colorado in September 1998. Although four-motor 500 series Dash 8-40BWs were bought for high-priority Super Fleet services, BNSF tended to assign the older four-motors to lower priority services as it acquired newer six-motor diesels. *Brian Solomon*

Among Santa Fe's hottest trains was Chicago–to–Richmond, California, symbol 199. On October 27, 1990, new Dash 8-40BW No. 513 leads 1-199-27 at McCook, Illinois, on the first leg of its westward journey. When new, Santa Fe's 500 series GEs were among the most intensively utilized locomotives in the United States. *Mike Abalos*

In April 1996, a pair of BNSF Dash 8-40BWs (also described as B40-8Ws) races westward on the old Chicago, Burlington & Quincy along the Mississippi River at Savanna, Illinois. *Brian Solomon*

Brand-new Santa Fe Dash 8-40CW No. 848 works west at Old Trojan on Ash Hill on June 12, 1992. Santa Fe's six-motor Dash 8s featured an unusual roof profile designed to accommodate dimensional constraints imposed by the coal-loading equipment at New Mexico's York Canyon mine. All Santa Fe 800 series locomotives, as well as many subsequent GE models, featured the nonstandard roof. *Brian Solomon*

Except for the North American Safety Cab, the Dash 8-40CW is essentially the same as the Dash 8-40C. Union Pacific No. 9475 works eastward with a K-Line double-stack east of Oxman, Oregon, on Encina Hill on July 12, 1993. *Brian Solomon*

A Union Pacific Dash 8-40CW works upgrade in the late afternoon at Paxton in California's Feather River Canyon on September 26, 1993. *Brian Solomon*

Conrail No. 6097 leads a westward freight near Mineral Point, Pennsylvania, on the old Pennsy main line on October 17, 1992. These locomotives were Conrail's first diesels with the North American Safety Cab (colloquially called the "widenose cab"), which has since become a standard feature on all new road freight diesels. The locomotive lacks ditch lights, now standard equipment that wasn't required when these locomotives were delivered in the early 1990s. *Brian Solomon*

Conrail Dash 8-40CW No. 6230, in fresh Conrail Quality paint, rolls west at Palmer, Massachusetts, on February 3, 1995. This rear view provides a good look at the Dash 8's radiator wings. In the 1990s, as GE increased engine output and was required to lower exhaust emissions, it increased the capacity of its radiator designs. The thinner radiator wings are an identifying feature of GE's older models. *Brian Solomon*

Conrail Dash 8-40CW No. 6118 leads eastward symbol freight BUOI (Buffalo, New York, to Oak Island, New Jersey) in deep snow on the former Erie Railroad at Rock Glen, New York, in January 1994. *Brian Solomon*

Right: This builder's plate was on a Chicago & North Western Dash 9-44CW constructed in April 1994. C&NW's Dash 9s were integrated into Union Pacific's fleet when UP absorbed the railroad in 1995. *Brian Solomon*

Below: A trio of new C&NW Dash 9-44CWs leads a Powder River Basin unit coal train through Creston, Illinois, on April 2, 1995. The Dash 9 era on C&NW was a short but colorful finale to the railroad's independent years. *Brian Solomon*

As a result of C&NW's unusual cab-signaling system, many of its former locomotives continued to work on former C&NW lines for several years after UP assumed control. On August 24, 1996, former C&NW Dash 9-44CW No. 8637 leads an eastward intermodal train on old home rails at Logan, Iowa. *Brian Solomon*

Designated Dash 9-44CWL, Canadian National's first Dash 9s were built in December 1994 (Nos. 2500–2522) and had a four-piece windshield instead of the two-piece design used in the United States. They were delivered with 70-mile-per-hour gearing but were limited to 65 miles per hour in Canada. This Dash 9 was photographed along the Mississippi River near Savanna, Illinois, on April 2, 1995. *Brian Solomon*

CN's later Dash 9s (Nos. 2523–2727), built as Dash 9-44CWs, use a variation of the two-piece windshield design. On June 14, 2004, No. 2680 leads a pair of EMD cowls northward at Lost Arrow Road in Byron, Wisconsin, on the former Wisconsin Central, which CN acquired in 2001. *Brian Solomon*

In 1994, Southern Pacific ordered Dash 9-44CWs that were assigned to a variety of heavy services, including iron ore trains operating from Minnesota's Iron Range to Geneva, Utah. In December 1994, a trio of new SP Dash 9s leads a taconite train on Wisconsin Central near Byron, Wisconsin. *Brian Solomon*

On September 11, 1994, a recently delivered Santa Fe Dash 9-44CW (known to the railroad as a C44-9W) leads a Union Equity unit train full of Kansas wheat on Santa Fe's Galveston Subdivision at Rosenburg, Texas. As in the case with Santa Fe's earlier six-motor safety cabs, their Dash 9s featured a distinctive cab roof profile. *Tom Kline*

New BNSF Dash 9-44CWs lead symbol freight S-CHIRIC (Stack–Chicago to Richmond, California) westward at Sugar Creek, Missouri, in August 1997. For almost two years after the 1995 BNSF merger, the new railroad continued to order a portion of its new power in Super Fleet paint, a variation of the scheme designed in the 1930s for Electro-Motive diesels built for the streamlined *Super Chief. Chris Guss*

Among the features made standard with the Dash 9 model was GE's new HiAd truck design, as seen on this new Santa Fe unit in 1994. *Brian Solomon*

BNSF Dash 9-44CWs lead a westward freight through the Feather River Canyon near Rich Bar, California, on August 15, 2009. *Brian Solomon*

This going-away view of the same train pictured on the facing page shows four BNSF Dash 9-44CWs approaching Rich Bar, California, with a long carload freight that originated at Pasco, Washington. At the back of this train are two additional Dash 9-44CWs working as distributed power units (DPUs), remotely controlled via radio from the head end. *Brian Solomon*

Dwarfed by massive basalt cliffs, a pair of BNSF Dash 9-44CWs leads an eastward unit grain train winding along Washington's Columbia River Gorge near Cooks Point on September 24, 2004. *Tom Kline*

Norfolk Southern was the only American railroad to order Dash 9s with a conventional cab—essentially the body style introduced with the older Dash models in the mid-1980s. In October 2001, NS No. 8771 leads an eastward intermodal train on the former Erie Railroad main line near Waverly, New York. *Brian Solomon*

Above and opposite: Norfolk Southern Dash 9-40C No. 8782 rolls eastward through Roanoke, Virginia, in October 2005. Like NS's Dash 9-40CW, the Dash 9-40C is rated at just 4,000 horsepower rather than 4,400 horsepower. By lowering the maximum output in the higher throttle notches, NS can better conserve fuel. *Brian Solomon*

A Norfolk Southern Dash 9-40CW races eastward on the old Pennsy main line near Mexico, Pennsylvania. NS Dash 9-40CWs use the same frame, HiAd trucks, 16-cylinder 7FDL engine, and 752AH-31 traction motors as the Dash 9-44CW. However, software in the locomotive's engine-governing unit rates the locomotive at 4,000 horsepower rather than the more common 4,400 horsepower. *Brian Solomon*

On July 19, 2009, NS Dash 9-40CW No. 9575 leads eastward unit coal train No. 532 on the former Erie Railroad main line east of Alfred, New York. NS sends coal trains and empties over the former Erie route between Meadville, Pennsylvania, and Hornell, New York. The section was closed to through traffic during the Conrail era, but was reopened in 2003 by short-line operator Western New York & Pennsylvania. *Brian Solomon*

This view of NS Dash 9-40CW No. 9764 at Roanoke, Virginia, offers a good look at the top of the cab and hood. Notice the second locomotive is painted only in primer. Later, after the locomotive entered service, it was given a fresh coat of NS paint. *Brian Solomon*

On July 20, 1995, against the backdrop of the Book Cliffs, a pair of new Southern Pacific AC4400CWs leads a unit taconite train west on the former Denver & Rio Grande Western main line in the Utah desert near Solitude. *Brian Solomon*

On July 18, 1995, a trio of new SP AC4400CWs leads an eastward unit coal train out of the tunnels at Kyune, Utah, on the former D&RGW/Utah Railway crossing of Soldier Summit. *Brian Solomon*

SP AC4400CW No. 101 eases a loaded taconite train downgrade through the Deen Tunnel near Pando, Colorado, on the former D&RGW crossing of Tennessee Pass. The line over the pass was among the steepest and highest in the United States before Union Pacific closed it in 1997. Freight movement over this route benefited only briefly from modern AC-traction diesels like this. *Brian Solomon*

Shortly before being absorbed by Union Pacific in spring 1995, Chicago & North Western took delivery of its last new locomotives: AC4400CWs that it assigned to Powder River Basin coal trains. C&NW No. 8810 is at Bill, Wyoming, in May 1995. Externally, the AC4400CW looks similar to the DC-traction Dash 9-44CW, except for the extended electrical cabinets housing the AC inverters behind the cab on the fireman's side. *Brian Solomon*

On the clear morning of July 12, 2005, Union Pacific AC4400CW No. 5922 leads a pair of EMD SD9043MACs eastbound at Troy, California, toward the famous Donner Summit on the old Southern Pacific. *Brian Solomon*

UP assigns its own locomotive model classifications, which often differ from the manufacturers' designations. According to UP, No. 5767 is a C44AC-CTE. The last three letters denote "controlled tractive effort," a feature that reduces maximum tractive effort for specific applications, such as work as DPUs. *Brian Solomon*

Above: CSX's 500 series AC4400CWs have an extra 10 tons of ballast to boost their tractive effort in slow-speed heavy service. Although originally assigned to coal trains on the old Baltimore & Ohio, in recent years 500 series AC4400CWs have been routinely assigned to service on the Boston Line in Massachusetts. No. 580 was photographed in fresh paint at Worcester, Massachusetts. *Brian Solomon*

Opposite top: At 11:36 a.m. on October 14, 2006, CSX Q116 drifts downgrade on the old Boston & Albany main line east of Becket, Massachusetts, at the Twin Ledges. No. 558 is one of CSX's heavy AC4400CWs featuring extra ballast. The trailing AC6000CW illustrates the difference in radiator profiles between the two diesels. *Brian Solomon*

Opposite bottom: CSX AC4400CW No. 588 and SD70MAC No. 4723 work west on the old West Shore Route across the bridge at French's Hollow, New York, on May 29, 2004. CSX identifies its AC-traction diesels with a lightning bolt below the road number. *Brian Solomon*

Kansas City Southern AC4400CWs Nos. 2011 and 2039 lead a southward grain train at Butlers Bluff, Missouri, on March 21, 2004. These AC4400CWs feature GE's steerable trucks, offered as an option in later years. Steerable trucks reduce friction in curves, thus minimizing wheel and rail wear while improving adhesion and fuel economy. The arrival of these locomotives in 1999 with distributed power capability brought an end to two of KCS's longstanding manned helper districts. *Chris Guss*

BNSF acquired a nominal fleet of production-built AC4400CWs before participating in GE's effort to advance the Evolution design. Built in late 2003 and early 2004, BNSF's prototypes were designated AC4400CWs and classed AC4400EV by BNSF. These were successful and BNSF ordered more than 600 production ES44ACs. *Chris Guss*

CP Rail AC4400CW No. 9635 works west with a loaded grain train near Lake Louise, Alberta, in August 1998. This is the typical power setup for CP Rail bulk trains operating in western Canada: two AC-traction locomotives on the head end and a third positioned approximately two-thirds back in the train. *Chris Guss*

In the mid-1990s Union Pacific ordered a fleet of locomotives from GE featuring the larger platform designed for the 6,000-horsepower AC6000CW but delivered with the older 4,400-horsepower 7FDL engine. UP later received a small fleet of true AC6000CWs powered by the 7HDL diesel, but the so-called "convertible" locomotives remained 4,400-horsepower machines and were known on the railroad as C6044ACs. *Brian Solomon*

A CSX AC6000CW works eastward through the Quaboag River Valley near West Warren, Massachusetts, on the former Boston & Albany main line. *Brian Solomon*

Opposite bottom: CSX bought the largest fleet of AC6000CWs. GE licensed design elements from German firm Deutz MWM, which were incorporated into the new four-cycle 7HDL. *Brian Solomon*

CSX No. 1, a GE AC4400CW, leads a loaded coal drag at the 21 Bridge east of Keyser, West Virginia, on October 17, 2002. Since buying its first AC4400CWs, CSX has assembled one of the largest fleets of AC-traction diesels in the United States. *Brian Solomon*

A rolling meet on the old Boston & Albany at milepost 130 finds CSX AC6000CW No. 689 leading an eastward train while brand-new ES44DCs work upgrade with Q119 (Boston to Chicago). Today, CSX operates a variety of modern GE six-motor diesels in heavy mainline service. *Brian Solomon*

On May 20, 2004, CSX AC4400CW No. 590 restrains an eastward train descending the Boston & Albany route near milepost 130. Improved dynamic braking is among the advantages offered by modern AC traction. *Brian Solomon*

BNSF is one of several American railroads to order separate fleets of AC- and DC-traction GE Evolution series locomotives. Externally, the locomotives appear almost the same, but their intended applications are distinct: AC locomotives are assigned to heavy service, such as coal trains, while DC locomotives are assigned to manifest and intermodal services. BNSF ES44DC No. 7649 leads an eastward freight on the former Western Pacific at Keddie, California, on August 15, 2009. *Brian Solomon*

This eastward CSX freight near Syracuse, Indiana, on June 14, 2010, provides a contrast in modern GE DC-traction diesels. Leading is CSX No. 5401, an ES44DC built new in 2007; trailing is a 1980s-era Dash 8-40C, among GE's first mass-produced microprocessor-controlled models. *Brian Solomon*

Canadian National ES44DC No. 2241 leads a pair of 1990s-era Dash 9-44CWs on the old Wisconsin Central just south of the Wisconsin–Illinois state line on June 15, 2010. CN has equipped its ES44DCs with distributed power and recently has expanded the use of this technology to include both older GEs and EMD SD70M-2s. *Brian Solomon*

Norfolk Southern ES40DC No. 7505 leads an empty hopper train west at Roanoke, Virginia, in October 2005. Like NS's Dash 9-40CWs, the railroad's Evolution series locomotives are rated at 4,000 horsepower rather than 4,400 to help conserve fuel. The change in output is accomplished electronically; mechanically, the two models are essentially the same. *Brian Solomon*

NS ES40DC No. 7505 was among the Evolution series prototypes built at Erie, Pennsylvania, in 2004, when the 1990s-era AC4400CW and Dash 9 models were still in regular production for domestic applications. The Evolution series supplanted the 1990s-era models when they entered full production in 2005. *Brian Solomon*

Norfolk Southern No. 7649 leads empty hopper train No. 691 westward on the former Pennsy Middle Division at Mexico, Pennsylvania, at 5:03 p.m. on July 1, 2010. This was one of 220 ES40DCs on the NS roster in July 2010. NS also has a fleet of 24 ES44ACs purchased in 2008 (Nos. 8000–8023). *Brian Solomon*

In May 2007, brand-new CSX ES44DC No. 5412 and AC4400CW No. 101 are down to a crawl with a heavy train of building debris on the former Boston & Albany west of Chester, Massachusetts. In October 2009, CSX started down-rating its ES44DCs to 4,000 horsepower and redesignating them ES40DCs. *Brian Solomon*

Above: CSX ES44DC No. 5211 is factory-fresh in this October 2, 2005, view at Stony Creek, Virginia, on the former Atlantic Coast Line main line. Trailing is another new Evolution series locomotive still wearing gray primer. *Brian Solomon*

Opposite: Among the distinct identifying characteristics of the Evolution series is the profile of extra-large radiator wings at the back of the locomotives. The Evolution series radiator package includes a state-of-the-art air-to-air heat exchanger and dual fans that allow the intercooler to lower engine gas emissions and extend life. *Brian Solomon*

BNSF ES44DC No. 7759 was only a few weeks out of GE's Erie, Pennsylvania, plant when it was photographed at Silo, New Mexico, on September 26, 2005. BNSF has ordered both AC and DC Evolutions for different applications; however, the success of the four-motor, six-axle ES44C4 may have the railroad focusing on AC types for future acquisitions. *Tom Kline*

Above: A BNSF westward freight works upgrade on the former Denver & Rio Grande Western at Thompson, Utah, on June 12, 2009. When Union Pacific absorbed Southern Pacific in 1996, BNSF acquired trackage rights on portions of the old D&RGW to maintain the guise of rail competition in the Central Corridor. BNSF No. 7284 was part of an order for 148 ES44DCs completed in the first three quarters of 2009. *Philip A. Brahms*

Opposite: On February 24, 2010, new BNSF Railway ES44DC No. 7297 leads a westward autorack train on the former Santa Fe at Collier, California. Notice the difference in the cab profile between the Evolution series, which has a standard GE cab roof, and the Dash 9s trailing behind with the specially designed cab roof specified by Santa Fe. *Philip A. Brahms*

Above: This rear view of BNSF ES44AC No. 5922 at Milano, Texas, offers an excellent perspective of the locomotive's HiAd trucks, 5,000-gallon fuel tanks, and extra-large radiator, which characterize the heavy appearance of the Evolution series. The defining equipment of the Evolution series, however, is concealed under the hood: GE's powerful and Tier II emissions-compliant GEVO-12 diesel engine. *Tom Kline*

Opposite: On August 15, 2009, new BNSF ES44ACs in fresh paint work west of Ottumwa, Iowa, with an intermodal train on the former Chicago, Burlington & Quincy main line. BNSF tends to send new coal power west from Chicago in groups like this. Once at Lincoln or Alliance, Nebraska, they can be placed in coal service. *Chris Guss*

The AC Motors decal applied to the HiAd truck on BNSF ES44AC No. 5921 is a reminder to shop forces accustomed to the common DC-traction motors on most of the fleet. GE offers its Evolution series in both AC- and DC-traction varieties. GE specs indicate that the ES44AC delivers 198,000 pounds of starting tractive effort compared to just 142,000 pounds on the ES44DC. The ES44AC can maintain 166,000 pounds of continuous tractive effort at very slow speeds; the ES44DC offers 109,000 pounds. *Tom Kline*

CP Rail ES44AC No. 8743 leads a southward freight on the old Delaware & Hudson at East Worcester, New York, on October 10, 2007. Since 2005, CP Rail has focused new locomotive acquisitions on the Evolution series AC-traction model. These are numbered in the 8700 and 8800 series and assigned to mainline freight services. *Brian Solomon*

Between Toronto, Ontario, and Binghamton, New York, CP traffic and locomotives run through as train Nos. 254 eastbound/255 westbound. On Norfolk Southern's former Erie Railroad trackage east of Buffalo, the trains operate with NS crews and carry NS symbols 38T eastbound/39T westbound. On February 11, 2010, ES44AC No. 8767 stirs up fresh powder at Dalton, New York, as it roars down the old Erie Railroad with 38T in tow. *Brian Solomon*

CP Rail ES44AC No. 8757 and an AC4400CW lead eastward train No. 198 on the former Milwaukee Road main line at Wepco, Wisconsin. Once famous for the fast-running *Hiawatha*, this route is now CP Rail's main line from western Canada and the Twin Cities to Chicago. While AC-traction locomotives really aren't needed in this flat terrain, CP prefers the flexibility of assigning its road units anywhere they're needed. *Chris Guss*

CSX empty autorack train Q293 climbs west on Washington Hill through pastoral scenery near Middlefield, Massachusetts, on October 17, 2009. ES44AC No. 945 was one of an order for 50 such locomotives in CSX's 900 series. Where CSX's ES44DCs are numbered in the 5200–5500 series, the AC-traction models carry three-digit numbers in the 700–900 series. *Brian Solomon*

CSX's ES44ACs feature steerable trucks instead of the more common GE HiAd trucks ordered on most new Evolution series locomotives. A variety of CSX AC-traction diesels have used the steerable truck, including its AC6000CW fleet and some of its AC4400CWs. *Brian Solomon*

Two CSX ES44ACs equipped with distributed power lead southbound utility coal across the Copper Creek Viaduct on the former Clinchfield near Speers Ferry, Virginia. A third ES44AC will be added to the rear of this train at Erwin, Tennessee, and linked via radio telemetry to operate as a remote locomotive. Operation of loaded coal trains with distributed power on the single-track former Clinchfield has eliminated a manned helper district and provided needed capacity to operate additional trains. *T. S. Hoover*

Above: Union Pacific ES44AC No. 5455 leads autoracks westward on the old Southern Pacific at Pinole, California, on August 26, 2009. UP, which doesn't employ GE's model designations, classifies this locomotive as a C45ACCTE. *Brian Solomon*

Opposite bottom: No. 2010, an experimental Evolution series hybrid, was displayed at Chicago on September 16, 2008. GE hopes to engineer modern hybrid technology using onboard batteries to store surplus energy generated during dynamic braking. While the technology is new, the concept is not: In the late 1920s GE built "tri-power" electric-diesels with banks of storage batteries, primarily for service on New York Central's electrified territory in New York City. *Chris Guss*

UP ES44AC No. 2010 was specially painted to commemorate the Boy Scouts of America centennial. It features the BSA logo on the side of the cab and merit badges on the walkway. The locomotive was photographed at an unveiling ceremony in Houston, Texas, on March 10, 2010, home to the largest troop council in the United States. *Tom Kline*

Today it's standard on the Union Pacific to operate locomotives as distributed power units. Radio-controlled DPU locomotives may be situated in the middle of a consist or at the back, reducing drawbar stress, lowering fuel consumption, improving train control, and eliminating most manned helper districts. On July 31, 2009, ES44AC No. 7918 leads a stack train on the former Western Pacific at Jungo, Nevada. Another ES44AC working as a DPU is situated at the rear of the train. *Brian Solomon*

Above: In the early morning of August 15, 2009, UP ES44AC No. 7635 leads a westward double-stack through the Feather River Canyon west of Virgilia, California. Forest fires burning in the Sierra filled the atmosphere with smoke and ash, lending an unusually rosy and dusty quality to the light. *Brian Solomon*

Opposite bottom: UP ES44AC No. 7412 catches the evening sun while working as a DPU at the back of a westward double-stack descending the former Western Pacific grade near Elsie, California, on August 14, 2009. *Brian Solomon*

Iowa Interstate Railroad (IAIS) ES44AC No. 512 bucks snow east of McClelland, Iowa, on the old Rock Island Chicago–Omaha main line. Unlike many smaller freight carriers that relied exclusively on second-hand locomotives, Iowa Interstate made the bold decision to purchase 12 state-of-the-art AC-traction Evolution series diesels to accommodate growing ethanol traffic. These were delivered in late 2008; in 2009, Iowa Interstate acquired two more units that were originally ordered by CSX. *Chris Guss*

Rock Island was liquidated in 1980, a decade before modern wide cabs were introduced, but this specially painted IAIS ES44AC leading a unit ethanol train at New Lenox, Illinois, in January 2010, offers a vision of what a modern Rock Island locomotive might have looked like. *Marshall W. Beecher*

IAIS acknowledges its Rock Island heritage by adapting the Rock Island herald. While many railroads have painted locomotives in heritage colors, in recent years only Iowa Interstate, Union Pacific, and Kansas City Southern have applied traditional paint to brand-new power.
Chris Guss

The ES44C4 is a six-axle, four-motor variation of the Evolution series. GE's locomotive test car divides a consist of four BNSF ES44C4s during a performance demonstration at Steward, Illinois, on March 12, 2009. The ES44C4 offers tractive and braking effort equivalent to a six-axle DC-propulsion locomotive while using four AC-traction motors on the number one, three, four, and six axles. AC-traction motors are more reliable and require less maintenance than the DC motors they replace. *Terry Norton*

The last light of October 29, 2008, paints the flanks of two Norfolk Southern ES44ACs pushing utility coal train No. 756 up the Elkhorn Grade at Elkhorn, West Virginia. NS's 24 NS ES44ACs feature additional ballast weight and, according to GE, have the greatest tractive and dynamic braking efforts of any commercially built diesel-electric locomotive. Because of this, they are ideally suited for helper assignments on the difficult grades of the Pocahontas Division. *T. S. Hoover*

One advantage of AC-traction systems is the ability to deliver substantially higher tractive effort. On November 6, 2008, a pair of nearly new NS ES44ACs working at full power assist utility coal train No. 762 in its ascent of the Elkhorn Grade on the former Norfolk & Western at Switchback, West Virginia. Since their arrival on the NS in 2008, pairs of ES44ACs have replaced sets of three DC six-axle locomotives as manned helper consists on the Pocahontas Division in Virginia and West Virginia. *T. S. Hoover*

Chapter 2
Electro-Motive Division

Electro-Motive Division

I n the 1970s, General Motors' Electro-Motive Division reigned as North America's leading locomotive manufacturer, a position it had held since the late 1940s. By the late 1970s, concerns with rising fuel costs, and greater fuel efficiency offered by General Electric's 7FDL engine, encouraged EMD to push its technology to new limits. While the 16-645E3 engine used to power its GP40-2 and SD40-2 locomotives had been rated at 3,000 horsepower, its new 16-645F3 engine was rated at 3,500 horsepower. To more effectively apply the increased output, EMD developed an improved wheel-slip control system called Super Series intended to boost wheel-rail adhesion. After producing a few experimental GP40Xs and SD40Xs that incorporated elements of its new technology, EMD introduced the 3,500-horsepower GP50 and SD50 production models (50 series) in 1981. (Horsepower was increased to 3,600 on later versions.) In addition to the new engine, these models employed the latest generation of electrical components. At 71 feet 2 inches, the SD50 was significantly longer than the SD40-2 that it supplanted as the builder's standard six-motor freight diesel.

Unfortunately, difficulties developed with locomotives powered by 16-645F engines. EMD refined a new engine block and developed an improved line of locomotives, known as its 60 series, using the new 710G engine derived from the 645 design, along with an improved electrical system incorporating microprocessors. In 1984, it began production of the six-motor 3,800-horsepower SD60, followed by the four-motor GP60 in 1985. The production of 50 series and 60 series locomotives overlapped by a couple of years while EMD perfected its new designs; externally, comparable models from the two series were similar in appearance.

Between 1987 and 1992, Electro-Motive implemented fundamental changes to its manufacturing process that resulted in the shifting of locomotive assembly for domestic sales from its La Grange, Illinois, plant to its London, Ontario–based Diesel Division. (In addition, some locomotive assembly was undertaken at other locations, including Conrail's Juniata Shops at Altoona, Pennsylvania, and at Super Steel in Schenectady, New York.)

Another change for EMD was the introduction and adoption of the modern

North American Safety Cab. Adapted from a Canadian cab design, the first application of the new cab style in the United States was on an order for Union Pacific SD60Ms that entered service during the early part of 1989. Initially, the SD60M used the safety cab configuration with a three-piece windshield as had been used for Canadian freight locomotives and the F59PH passenger diesel. Later locomotives utilized a refined design with a slightly tapered cab and a two-piece windshield. During the 1990s, EMD's safety cab design evolved. One variation was the whisper cab, sometimes referred to as an isolated cab because of its design that isolated the cab frame from the underframe superstructure. By the early 1990s, most railroads had adopted the safety cab, which has since become standard on all new freight locomotives.

In the 1990s, EMD introduced new locomotive lines for heavy-freight service. Its SD70 series made its debut in late 1992. The 4,000-horsepower SD70M represented a refinement of existing technology rather than a major change to primary components. By contrast, the SD70MAC, which made its debut a year later, ushered in a fundamental change in locomotive design. This was America's first commercially successful, heavy-haul diesel using a state-of-the-art three-phase alternating current traction system. Developed with German manufacturer Siemens, this system was applied experimentally to a pair of F69PHACs demonstrated on Amtrak in the early 1990s and then on four SD60MACs tested on Burlington Northern. BN was EMD's first major customer for AC traction. Superior traction characteristics allowed BN to assign three 4,000-horsepower SD70MAC units in place of five conventional 3,000-horsepower DC-traction units in Powder River coal service in Wyoming.

EMD continued to offer DC-traction models and sold several variations of its SD70, including the aforementioned SD70M, a conventional-cab model designated simply as an SD70 (bought by Norfolk Southern and Illinois Central), a whisper cab model SD70I, and uprated 4,300-horsepower variations designated SD75M and SD75I to Santa Fe/BNSF and Canadian National, respectively.

In the mid-1990s, EMD engineered its 6,000-horsepower SD90MAC-H and a convertible variation often known as an SD9043MAC (in effect, an SD70MAC capable of being upgraded to SD90MAC-H specs). Significantly, for the 6,000-horsepower model, EMD needed to develop an entirely new diesel engine, the four-cycle 265H, in order to generate 6,000 horsepower.

In the past decade, Electro-Motive engineered improvements to its locomotive line to comply with EPA emissions standards.

Previous pages:
Indiana Rail Road (INRD) is among the smaller railroads that operate modern high-horsepower Electro-Motive diesels, with 11 of them on the roster as of 2010. Most INRD coal trains can be operated with two SD9043MACs rather than three SD40-2s, saving maintenance and fuel costs. The SD9043MAC had only three customers for the 410 units produced: Union Pacific, Canadian National, and CIT Group, with the INRD units coming from the CIT order. *Chris Guss*

Reflecting these changes, it brought out its latest freight diesels in 2005: the DC-traction SD70M-2 and AC-traction SD70ACe. Also in that year, General Motors sold EMD to a consortium of Greenbriar Equity and Berkshire Partners. The initials EMD today stand for Electro-Motive Diesel. In 2010, EMD changed ownership again when it was sold to Caterpillar subsidiary Progress Rail Services. The company continues to manufacture its SD70M-2/SD70ACe lines, models that are virtually indistinguishable on the outside but have different performance characteristics—and different price tags.

Two Conrail SD80MACs, Nos. 4127 and 4116, glide eastward with autorack train ML-482 at Muddy Pond just east of Washington Summit near Hinsdale, Massachusetts. *Brian Solomon*

Above: Vermont Railway briefly operated two GP60s built for the Texas-Mexican Railway. On February 18, 2002, train No. 263, running from Rutland to Bellows Falls, Vermont, has freshly painted GP60 No. 381 in the lead as it ascends the grade to Mount Holly. *Brian Solomon*

Opposite top: Burlington Northern GP50 No. 3141 leads a westward intermodal train at East Dubuque, Illinois, in June 1995. The GP50 was the successor to the very popular GP40/GP40-2. Rated at 3,500 horsepower, it was powered by the 16-645F engine. Few railroads bought GP50s, and only a handful remain active in mainline service. *Brian Solomon*

Opposite bottom: Among EMD's more unusual modern four-axle models was the GP59, which only Norfolk Southern bought new. On October 17, 2008, NS No. 4616 works local freight H2R on the former Erie Railroad at Silver Springs, New York. Similar in appearance to the more common GP60, the GP59 was intended for high-horsepower applications and powered by a fuel-efficient 12-cylinder 710G engine rated at 3,000 horsepower compared with the GP60's 3,800 horsepower. *Brian Solomon*

Above: Southern Pacific GP60 No. 9746 leads a westward intermodal train destined for Oakland along the shores of San Pablo Bay at Pinole, California. SP was the largest buyer of the GP60, acquiring nearly 200 units for itself and its Cotton Belt and Denver & Rio Grande Western affiliates. *Brian Solomon*

Opposite top: SP's last new four-motor diesels were 25 3,800-horsepower GP60s built between November 1993 and January 1994. Photographed at Wendel, California, on February 11, 1994, No. 9789 was only weeks old. It was assigned to work a manifest freight on the remote Modoc Line between Klamath Falls, Oregon, and a connection with Union Pacific's former Western Pacific line at Flannigan, Nevada. *Brian Solomon*

This is a Blomberg truck on SP No. 9789. SP's GP60s used 70:17 gearing for fast intermodal work. Typical EMD road locomotives built between the 1970s and early 1990s used 62:18 gearing designed for a maximum operating speed of 65 miles per hour. By the time SP received its last GP60s, high-horsepower six-motor diesels were standard road freight locomotives in North America. *Brian Solomon*

Norfolk Southern SD50 No. 6522 leads eastward intermodal No. 168 on CP Rail's Delaware & Hudson route at Nineveh, New York, on October 13, 2003. This SD50 wasn't making points with the railroad; it wasn't loading properly and as a result the train stalled climbing Belden Hill out of Binghamton, New York. A following CP Rail train shoved 168 to the top of the hill and from that point on a trailing NS GE-built Dash 9-40CW moved 168 eastward to Albany. *Brian Solomon*

Canadian National bought a cowl body type variation of the SD50 designated SD50F. Sixty were built by EMD affiliate GMD at London, Ontario, between 1985 and 1987. Like other late-era SD50s, they were powered by the 16-645F3B engine rated at 3,600 horsepower and geared for 65 miles per hour. No. 5434 leads a southward freight on the former Wisconsin Central near Church Road in Byron, Wisconsin, on June 22, 2004. *Brian Solomon*

The SD50 resulted from EMD's efforts to improve upon its popular 1970s-era SD40-2. Regular production began in 1981, and the design was originally rated at 3,500 horsepower; later production SD50s were upped to 3,600 horsepower. All were powered by the 16-645F diesel and used state-of-the-art D87 traction motors. Due to perceived design flaws, the locomotives have been compared unfavorably with the SD40-2. On June 28, 1996, Union Pacific No. 5011 leads Conrail empty hopper train UNW-417 on Conrail trackage at Hammond, Indiana. *Mike Abalos*

Opposite top: Norfolk Southern SD40Es shove a loaded unit coal train toward the summit of the Alleghenies at Gallitzin, Pennsylvania, on June 30, 2010. The SD40E designation for NS's rebuilt 1980s-era SD50s reflects the work done to them, with the "E" inferring "enhanced" and describing the modern electrical system that provides greater tractive effort than available from a conventional SD40-2. NS evaluated eight microprocessor controls before choosing EMD's EM2000 system. *Brian Solomon*

Opposite bottom: One of CSX's rebuilt SD50 models—SD50-3 No. 8526—works eastward on the former Baltimore & Ohio main line near Nappanee, Indiana, on June 14, 2010. CSX's constituent railroads, Chessie System and Seaboard System, placed significant orders for SD50s in the mid-1980s. *Brian Solomon*

Right: On July 1, 2010, a pair of NS SD40Es shoves on the back of a heavy westward freight at Gallitzin, Pennsylvania. NS has rebuilt a number of former Conrail SD50s, as SD40Es, downgrading the 3,500-horsepower 16-645F engine to a 3,000-horsepower 16-645E3C configuration and replacing the electrical system with modern microprocessor controls. In 2010, the rebuilding program was still underway and expected to result in a 54-unit fleet of manned helpers. *Brian Solomon*

Above: An SD60 leads a Norfolk Southern RoadRailer westward on the old Wabash near Attica, Indiana, on October 20, 2002. The SD60 was an improvement on the SD50, employing the new 16-710G engine and microprocessor controls. Variations of the SD60 include the SD60M with a North American Safety Cab, the SD60I with an isolated cab to reduce noise, and Canadian National's SD60F with a cowl body style. *Brian Solomon*

Opposite top: On September 20, 1989, new Conrail SD60s work west with train TV201X, carrying K-Line containers on the former New York Central Water Level Route at Dunkirk, New York. Computer controls in the 60 series diesel allowed more precise regulation of engine and electrical components, controlled main generator excitation, and provided detailed computerized diagnostic systems for more effective analysis of performance flaws. *Brian Solomon*

On July 12, 1994, Oakway SD60 No. 9002 works an empty coal train westward on Burlington Northern's former Northern Pacific main line near Sentinel Butte in the North Dakota Badlands. Oakway provided BN with a "power by the hour" fleet of 100 SD60s. *Brian Solomon*

Burlington Northern SD60Ms lead an eastward CP Rail freight on the former Milwaukee Road just south of downtown Milwaukee, Wisconsin, on July 8, 1995. No. 9254 is representative of later SD60Ms that featured a two-piece windshield and a slightly tapered nose section. The early SD60Ms had an untapered, boxier nose and a three-piece windshield. *Brian Solomon*

On July 27, 1991, Union Pacific SD60M No. 6255 leads a westward freight upgrade on Encina Hill near Oxman, Oregon. Two SD40-2s work as manned helpers at the back. UP's first SD60Ms entered service in early 1989, 20 years after UP's famous DDA40X Centennials, which featured the 1960s version of a wide-nose cab. *Brian Solomon*

On May 22, 1993, UP SD60M No. 6172 works eastward through the Feather River Canyon on the former Western Pacific main line. Known in some circles as "Cyclops" for their distinctive appearance, SD60Ms were commonly assigned to lead UP freights on this route in the early 1990s. *Brian Solomon*

Conrail SD60I leads intermodal train TV6 eastward at the Twin Ledges east of Becket, Massachusetts, at 10:03 a.m. on May 24, 1997. Conrail operated both SD60Ms and SD60Is. The latter featured the noise-reducing whisper cab (a.k.a. isolated cab) and was assembled at the railroad's Juniata Shops in Altoona, Pennsylvania. *Brian Solomon*

On July 1, 2010, three former Conrail SD60Is leading westward coal-hopper train No. 643 at Cassandra, Pennsylvania, descend the western slope of the former Pennsylvania Railroad's Allegheny crossing. Because of tight clearances on the rotary car dumper at Pennsylvania Power & Light's Strawberry Ridge power plant, dedicated locomotives are assigned to Norfolk Southern's PP&L unit trains. In recent years the railroad has used SD60Is in three-unit sets. *Brian Solomon*

On February 20, 2004, CSX SD60I No. 8731 rolls across the trestle at Weldon, North Carolina, on the former Atlantic Coast Line main line. This angle offers a view of the metal separating the cab and the front of the locomotive nose, which is an identifying feature of EMD's whisper cab and distinguishes the SD60M from the SD60I. *Brian Solomon*

On May 27, 1991, five GP60Ms lead hot Santa Fe intermodal No. 1-198-27 at McCook, Illinois. Six-motor units with North American Safety Cabs became standard on U.S. main lines in the 1990s, but only Santa Fe ordered modern four-motor units with this cab design for high-speed intermodal service. The GP60M and cabless GP60B were unique to Santa Fe and, after 1995, Santa Fe's successor, BNSF. *Mike Abalos*

In October 1990, a nearly new Santa Fe GP60M leads a westward intermodal train through California's Glen Frazer Canyon. The high-horsepower four-motor diesels were standard power on trains to and from Richmond, California. *Brian Solomon*

A trio of Santa Fe GP60Ms races eastward with a stack train in New Mexico in January 1994. In the late 1980s, Santa Fe worked with GM and GE to design the North American Safety Cab as part of its concessions to reduce crew sizes and lengthen crew districts. The new cab had its origins in designs used by Canadian lines and was intended to reduce engine noise; provide desktop controls, giving the engineer a forward-facing position; and provide greater structural safety in the event of a collision. *Brian Solomon*

In the 1990s, Illinois Central bucked the trends toward AC traction, North American Safety Cabs, and other innovations by ordering very basic SD70s. A pair of these race northward on IC's main line in central Illinois on June 23, 2004. By then, IC was part of the Canadian National system. *Brian Solomon*

IC received 40 SD70s from EMD in 1995 (Nos. 1000–1039). It was one of just three railroads to receive this conventional-cab model. The class leader was on display at Homewood, Illinois, in October 1995. *Brian Solomon*

Illinois Central SD70 No. 1008 basks in the glow of sodium vapor lights reflecting off snow at Genoa, Illinois. Powered by EMD's successful 16-710G3B engine, the SD70 was rated at 4,000 horsepower. Only 120 conventional-cab SD70s were built, making them rare among the more than 1,600 SD70 series locomotives built with variations of the North American Safety Cab. *Chris Guss*

Above: In May 2002, Norfolk Southern SD70s Nos. 2578 and 2582 are virtually spotless as they approach South Fork, Pennsylvania, with a five-car company business train. *Brian Solomon*

Opposite bottom: Conrail's last locomotives were ordered by its new owners, CSX and Norfolk Southern, but delivered in Conrail paint. The 2500 series SD70s were built to NS specifications, including a conventional cab and control stand. By contrast, CSX ordered SD70MACs. Here, new Conrail SD70s work west between Spruce Creek and Union Furnace, Pennsylvania, in November 1998. Six months later this route became part of the NS system. *Brian Solomon*

NS SD70 No. 2561 leads an empty Mount Tom coal train westward on Guilford Rail System's Boston & Maine route at Eagle Bridge, New York, in October 2001. *Brian Solomon*

SD70M demonstrators made their rounds on Southern Pacific in June 1993, painted in EMD's latest demonstrator scheme. The primary difference between the SD70M and the SD70 was the cab style. *Brian Solomon*

SP's last new EMDs—and its only EMDs with North American Safety Cabs—were 25 units purchased in 1994. Initially, many of these were assigned to work between Portland, Oregon, and Los Angeles on the so-called I-5 Corridor. In June 1994, new SP No. 9808 was photographed on a freight in Loring, Kansas, on Union Pacific trackage rights. In Topeka, the train would switch to home rails for the trip west. *Chris Guss*

Norfolk Southern operates several variations of the SD70, including conventional-cab SD70s, early- and late-era SD70Ms, and the more modern SD70M-2. This eastward freight at Lilly, Pennsylvania, on June 23, 2006, demonstrates the difference in radiator profiles between the leading SD70M and the trailing SD70M-2. *Brian Solomon*

Union Pacific No. 3934 is a long way from home rails on October 17, 2008, as it leads an eastward CSX freight on the former New York Central Water Level Route at Upton Road in Batavia, New York. UP bought large numbers of SD70Ms in the early 2000s. Today this model remains the most common locomotive on the railroad. *Brian Solomon*

This view of a westward UP freight at James, California, offers an excellent comparison of the different radiator profiles of three modern EMD locomotives. In the lead is an SD90/43MAC with the large radiator designed for EMD's 265H engine (although the locomotive is powered by a 16-710G3B). It is followed by one of UP's late-era SD70Ms with gently angled radiator intakes and an early-era SD70M with a conventional radiator profile. Increasingly stringent EPA emissions requirements have been met, in part, by increasing radiator capacity. *Brian Solomon*

In 1999, Union Pacific ordered 1,000 "retro" SD70Ms. Instead of modern desktop electronics, these featured conventional analog engineer controls and other low-tech equipment, such as mechanical fuel injection in place of electronic fuel injection. On Halloween Day 2003, UP No. 4209 was working toward Donner Summit with a westbound freight when it crawled past Old Gorge east of Alta, California. Lost in the fog is the American River, some 2,000 feet lower than rail level. *Brian Solomon*

On June 24, 1996, Canadian National SD70I No. 5603 winds through Steward, Illinois, westbound on BNSF's former Chicago, Burlington & Quincy line between Chicago and the Twin Cities. In the mid-1990s CN ordered a fleet of 4,000-horsepower SD70Is followed by 4,300-horsepower SD75Is. Both featured EMD's isolated whisper cab. Because output was adjusted with software changes, there were no differentiating external features between the two models, except for slight changes to the paint schemes. *Brian Solomon*

CN SD75I No. 5788 works west on the main line at Coteau, Quebec, on October 23, 2004. One way to quickly spot the difference between CN's SD70I and SD75I (as built) is the larger CN logo on the SD75Is, which extends above the handrails. *Brian Solomon*

For a few years in the mid-1990s, CN routed traffic between Duluth, Minnesota, and Chicago over Burlington Northern (BNSF after 1995) routes. Later, CN shifted its traffic to a Wisconsin Central routing in a prelude to CN's acquisition of that line. In July 1996, an eastward CN freight rolls toward Steward, Illinois, with a relatively new SD70I. *Brian Solomon*

New BNSF SD75Ms work west of Craig, Kansas, in February 1996. EMD's SD75M was a variation of the SD70M that uses the same hardware but uses software to deliver 4,300 horsepower instead of 4,000. These two extra-clean locomotives arrived the previous night on an executive business car special from Phoenix, Arizona. *Chris Guss*

This SD75M was the very last new locomotive delivered to Santa Fe Railway before its amalgamation into BNSF in September 1995. *Brian Solomon*

In 1995, Santa Fe ordered SD75Ms for Super Fleet intermodal services, such as No. 207, photographed at Corwith Yard, Chicago, on July 2, 1995. New SD75Ms early in the BNSF era were dressed in Santa Fe's war bonnet paint with BNSF lettering on the sides and "Santa Fe" in the front herald. *Brian Solomon*

Burlington Northern was first to order EMD's pioneering commercial heavy-haul, three-phase AC-traction diesel. Although BN/BNSF acquired SD70MACs specifically for Power River Basin coal traffic, AC-traction diesel-electric locomotives occasionally wander from the coal pool to other services. In October 2002, a pair of BNSF SD70MACs leads a CSX freight past vintage General Railway Signal semaphores on the former Monon at Romney, Indiana. *Brian Solomon*

Above: BNSF SD70MACs lead a Powder River Coal train on September 13, 2008. Key to the SD70MAC design is a pair of high-voltage inverters that convert DC power to modulated AC used for traction. Railroads are keen to use AC-traction locomotives in heavy service because modern AC motors allow for significantly greater tractive effort while requiring less maintenance and are not at risk from overloading. *Philip A. Brahms*

Opposite bottom: In the fading light of February 1997, a trio of BNSF SD70MACs in their as-delivered Grinstein Green (so named for BN chairman Gerald Grinstein) and cream paint work a loaded coal train toward Colorado's Palmer Divide. The ability of three AC-traction SD70MACs to replace five traditional 3,000-horsepower DC-traction diesels in coal service offered BN a substantial cost savings that encouraged the railroad to place a significant order for the new type. Although AC technology was not a new concept, EMD needed to adapt European AC-traction systems to the rigors of American freight railroading. *Brian Solomon*

New CSX SD70MACs leading a loaded coal train eastward meet SD50 No. 8552 working west at Cumberland, Maryland, on September 25, 1997. Locomotive No. 712 was from the first of several CSX orders for SD70MACs. CSX assigned its first SD70MACs to coal service on former Baltimore & Ohio lines, while later locomotives were bought for more varied duties around the system. *Brian Solomon*

On April 6, 2004, new CSX SD70MAC No. 4765 and an AC6000CW leading an eastward freight have just passed Washington Summit in the Berkshires of western Massachusetts. CSX's later SD70MACs featured tapered radiators with a greater cooling surface necessary to comply with more stringent emissions requirements. *Brian Solomon*

A pair of SD70MACs working west with an empty autorack train Q283 ascend the former Boston & Albany grade over Washington Hill near milepost 129 on October 5, 2007. CSX No. 4709 lacks its identifying nose herald. *Brian Solomon*

Above: Kansas City Southern No. 3905 leads train IJALZ-28 (Intermodal–Jackson, Mississippi, to Lazaro Cardenas, Mexico) north of Lucas, Louisiana, on April 28, 2008. To better align the motive power needs of the new KCS system, former TFM SD70MACs were reassigned to the KCS property in the United States while the KCS SD60s were sent to Mexico. The AC-traction locomotives are better suited for graded territory south of Kansas City. *Chris Guss*

Opposite top: TFM No. 1602 is part of a distributed power consist on the rear of a KCS coal empty just south of Anderson, Missouri. Over the years, KCS has tried manned helpers and remote-controlled consists over its two major grades, but AC-traction locomotives and distributed power have become KCS's new standard for moving tonnage on this busy Midwest corridor. *Chris Guss*

Opposite bottom: KCS No. 3920 started life as TFM No. 1620, but now wears its new reporting marks as it undergoes an overhaul at KCS' Shreveport, Louisiana, shops. It and the other 74 TFM SD70MACs will receive the same treatment as they begin their second life hauling tonnage in the Midwest after a decade of service in Mexico. TFM was one of six railroads that ordered the SD70MAC over the model's 11-year production span. *Chris Guss*

Only Conrail bought the SD80MAC, and it acquired 30 of the 5,000-horsepower model in the mid-1990s. Powered by a 20-cylinder 710G3 diesel, these big locomotives were the railroad's first AC-traction locomotives and briefly held the title as America's most powerful single-engine, single-unit diesel electrics. On August 30, 1997, a pair of SD80MACs and a pair of GE B23-7s work east of Hinsdale, Massachusetts, near Washington Summit with a heavy eastward freight. *Brian Solomon*

New Conrail SD80MAC No. 4104 leads an eastward freight past the Twin Ledges east of Becket, Massachusetts, in October 1996. In Conrail's final years, it routinely assigned pairs of SD80MACs to Boston Line freights. When CSX assumed operations of this route in 1999, the 20-cylinder EMDs were largely reassigned to other duties. *Brian Solomon*

The SD80MAC measured 80 feet 2 inches long, weighed approximately 430,000 pounds fully serviceable, and could deliver 185,000 pounds starting tractive effort. When CSX and Norfolk Southern divided Conrail in 1999, each inherited some of the unique SD80MAC fleet. NS has primarily assigned its locomotives to coal service out of South Fork, Pennsylvania. On June 24, 2006, NS No. 7203 works a coal train at Summerhill, Pennsylvania. *Brian Solomon*

EMD's 6,000-horsepower locomotive was delayed while it refined its 265H engine. In the interim, it offered the "upgradeable" SD9043MAC, delivered with the older 16-710G3B engine rated at 4,300 horsepower. CP Rail No. 9125 leads an eastward intermodal at Boston Bar, British Columbia, on August 10, 1999. Due to costs and logistical issues, none of the convertible locomotives were ever upgraded. *Chris Guss*

Above: To achieve 6,000 horsepower with a single-engine locomotive, EMD introduced its four-cycle 265H engine—model GM16V265—to power the SD90MAC-H. In practice these locomotives were less common than the similar-looking SD9043MAC upgradeable types. Union Pacific SD90MAC-H No. 8535 was at Chicago's Clearing Yard diesel shop on June 30, 2000. *Chris Guss*

Opposite bottom: To avoid confusion between the 4,300-horsepower variation and the true 6,000-horsepower locomotive, various designations have been used for the "upgradeables," including SD9043MAC, SD90/43MAC, and SD9043AC. Both CP Rail and Union Pacific ordered upgradeable and new 6,000-horsepower variations. In July 2005, near Troy, California, a GE leads a pair of UP SD9043ACs working east toward Donner Summit. *Brian Solomon*

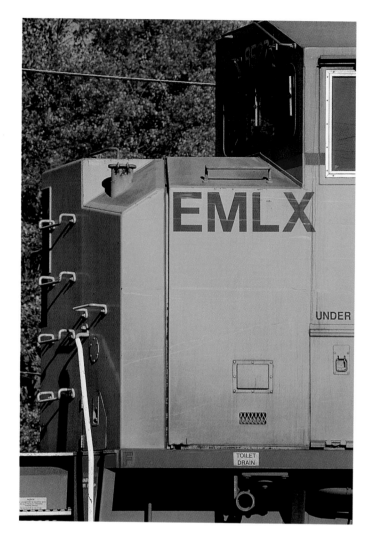

EMD's modern cab was introduced during production of UP's SD90MAC-H. While some of the locomotives featured the new cab, others featured the older style of North American Safety Cab introduced in the early 1990s for use on the SD60 and applied to the SD9043AC "upgradeables." Today, the modern angular cab style is standard on both the SD70M-2 and SD70ACe. *Brian Solomon*

Opposite top: Genesee & Wyoming short line Buffalo & Pittsburgh was among the last railroads to operate SD90MAC-Hs in heavy freight service. A pair of former Union Pacific SD90MAC-Hs leased by EMLX leads B&P's southward freight at East Salamanca, New York, on October 18, 2008. *Brian Solomon*

Opposite bottom: Former UP No. 8527 leads a B&P freight on October 11, 2008. The 6,000-horsepower SD90MAC-H was among the most interesting, although unsuccessful, modern diesels. Compared with other models, the majority of SD90MAC-Hs had very short service lives—the unusual engine and reported lower-than-anticipated availability, combined with the nonstandard horsepower rating, contributed to their early retirement. Most of the big units have been scrapped. *Brian Solomon*

Above: On August 14, 2009, a westward Union Pacific double-stack passes the siding at Elsie, Oregon, on the former Western Pacific. This broadside image offers a good comparison between the SD70ACe (leading) and an upgradeable SD9043AC. The SD70ACe is just 74 feet 3 inches long, compared to 80 feet 2 inches. Both locomotives have AC traction and are rated at 4,300 horsepower, but the ACe is a more modern design built to comply with the more stringent EPA Tier 2 emissions requirements. *Brian Solomon*

Opposite top: UP SD70ACe No. 8341 rolls east through Colfax, California, with a train ascending toward Donner Pass. Since 2005, the SD70ACe has been EMD's standard AC-traction freight locomotive. The small letter "e" in the designation stands for "enhanced," reflecting changes to the engine design. *Brian Solomon*

Opposite bottom: On May 6, 2010, UP SD70ACe No. 1995 leads the company business train near Canal Street in Chicago. This is one of several locomotives dressed in special heritage liveries resembling paint schemes used by railroads absorbed by Union Pacific. UP melded the old Chicago & North Western into its system in 1995. *Chris Guss*

CSX SD70ACe No. 4834 and an SD70MAC drift downgrade with an eastward freight on the old Boston & Albany main line east of Middlefield, Massachusetts, on May 4, 2007. EMD specifications indicate an SD70ACe offers 106,000 pounds braking effort, compared with just 86,850 pounds on the SD70M-2. Externally the two locomotives look almost identical—the primary difference is their AC and DC traction systems. *Brian Solomon*

In October 2005, a nearly new CSX SD70ACe leads an eastward freight by the former Boston & Albany passenger station at Warren, Massachusetts. Seventy-nine years earlier, New York Central's B&A invested in extremely powerful Lima 2-8-4 steam locomotives, named Berkshires in honor of the line. Where a Class A1a 2-8-4 offered 81,400 pounds tractive effort with a booster, today's SD70ACe can deliver 191,000 pounds. *Brian Solomon*

CSX SD70ACe No. 4809 works singly with a southward freight past the Richmond, Virginia, Amtrak station on the former Richmond, Fredericksburg & Potomac in early October 2005. *Brian Solomon*

Three-phase AC traction made its debut in Powder River coal service on BNSF predecessor Burlington Northern. Today, BNSF continues to buy the most modern AC-traction diesels for this same service. On September 27, 2009, BNSF SD70ACe No. 9355 leads a loaded unit train on the Orin Line south of Gillette, Wyoming. *Patrick Yough*

BNSF SD70ACe No. 9206 catches the afternoon sun under a big sky on September 28, 2009. The advent of distributed power technology has changed the way BNSF assigns locomotives to heavy trains. Where in 1994, three SD70MACs would have led a loaded unit coal train, today it is typical for two modern ACs to lead and one to work as a radio-controlled DPU at the back of the train. BNSF operates approximately 80 percent of its unit coal trains with DPUs. *Patrick Yough*

BNSF SD70ACe No. 9230 shows off its fresh paint. *Patrick Yough*

Kansas City Southern SD70ACe No. 4115 leads a unit grain extra north of Rich Mountain, Arkansas, on April 27, 2008. *Chris Guss*

In the early 2000s, KCS began ordering freight diesels in a paint scheme that was a close adaptation of its 1940s-era streamliner, *Southern Belle*. On April 29, 2008, SD70ACe No. 4108 and a new General Electric ES44AC lead a unit grain train at DeQuincy, Louisiana. *Chris Guss*

As spring foliage begins to emerge, KCS SD70ACe No. 4013 leads an intermodal train north of Hatton, Arkansas. Rated at 4,300 horsepower, a single SD70ACe has sufficient power to move a relatively light train. *Chris Guss*

On June 13, 2008, a new pair of Montana Rail Link SD70ACe diesels lead westward freight LM (Laurel to Missoula) out of the west portal of the summit tunnel on Mullen Pass. This former Northern Pacific crossing of the Continental Divide is operated by MRL today but still carries a considerable volume of BNSF through freight. *Tom Kline*

MRL SD70Ace locomotives are head-end helpers leading a westward BNSF loaded coal train on the Austin Creek Trestle at Austin, Montana, toward the summit of the Continental Divide. Until its acquisition of 16 SD70ACe locomotives in 2005, MRL operated its entire railroad with second-hand diesels, including a substantial fleet of EMDs powered by the 1960s-era 20-645E3 engine rated at 3,600 horsepower. *Tom Kline*

In the final twinkle of sun on the western side of the Continental Divide, Montana Rail Link SD70ACe No. 4301 rolls downgrade with the Laurel-to-Missoula symbol freight LM. MRL's 16 SD70ACe locomotives are numbered 4300–4315. *Tom Kline*

New Norfolk Southern SD70M-2 No. 2667 works westward and catches the attention of visitors at Pennsylvania's famous Horseshoe Curve on June 23, 2006. Today this modern diesel does the job once performed by Pennsylvania Railroad's massive steam locomotives. *Brian Solomon*

NS SD70M-2 No. 2735 leads eastward intermodal train No. 168 on Canadian Pacific's Delaware & Hudson route near Worcester, New York, on October 10, 2007. NS has opted to purchase EMD's DC-traction diesels rather than the more expensive AC-traction models. *Brian Solomon*

Canadian National has not embraced the AC-traction trend. Instead it has purchased DC-traction models exclusively from both General Electric and EMD in recent years. On September 9, 2009, SD70M-2 No. 8805 leads train 406 at Rothesay, New Brunswick.
George S. Pitarys

Chapter 3
Passenger Locomotives

Passenger Locomotives

While passenger locomotives are highly specialized designs representing only a small portion of locomotives manufactured, people tend to be more familiar with these locomotives than the hoards of heavy-haul freight diesels. Where the 410 SD9043MACs in freight service seem relatively unusual to the casual observer, the 207 P42DC Genesis locomotives built for Amtrak are emblematic of contemporary U.S. intercity passenger operations.

Compared with freight diesels, where a few standard types ordered in large numbers to nearly identical specifications satisfy the bulk of the market, passenger locomotives tend to be tailored to individual buyer specifications and purchased in small batches. Complicating the passenger locomotive business is the fact that most essential North American locomotive technologies have been developed and refined for the demands of the more lucrative freight locomotive business. The result is that locomotive technology must be adapted at relatively high cost to the specific services demanded by passenger applications. In the 1960s, 1970s, and 1980s, passenger locomotives were derived from freight models, with only very slight changes, such as the addition of head-end electrical power for heating and lighting trains. Since the 1990s, while primary components for passenger locomotives have been essentially the same as those for freight diesels, locomotive configuration has blended American and European technologies in an effort to produce machines better suited to passenger services.

Traditionally, passenger locomotives have been built by the same firms that focus on freight locomotives; since the 1960s this has largely been EMD and GE. During the 1980s and 1990s, remanufactured locomotives for passenger applications were developed by several smaller manufacturers, such as MotivePower's predecessor, MK Rail. Since 2000, changes in the locomotive marketplace, predicated by ever stricter environmental controls, have resulted in the commercial obsolescence of EMD's and GE's established passenger types, leaving the market open to smaller builders.

When Amtrak sought to replace its fleet of aging 1970s-era Electro-Motive F40PHs in the 1990s, it was unwilling to settle for adaptations of existing freight locomotives.

Among the most interesting diesels in North America are NJ Transit's 33 PL42-ACs built by Alstom at the former Erie Railroad shops in Hornell, New York. These are a unique melding of European and North American technologies unlike anything operating on either continent. They are powered by an EMD 16-710G3B-T1 diesel and rated at 4,200 horsepower. Atypical of North American diesels is their unusual European-style traction system. *Patrick Yough*

GE and EMD placed bids for a modern, lightweight, state-of-the-art locomotive, with GE winning the contract. GE worked with Amtrak in the design, incorporating several European concepts. GE designated the resulting type as its Genesis line. Among the distinct characteristics of the Genesis are fabricated trucks in place of conventional cast-steel trucks and a monocoque body shell that's integral with the locomotive structure, rather than a nonstructural covering atop a platform.

GE developed three Genesis models. The first was the 4,000-horsepower Dash 8-40BP (sometimes known as the P40), of which 44 were built for Amtrak numbered in

Previous pages:
Amtrak F59PHI with a *Pacific Surfliner* at San Diego in June 2008 represents modern passenger locomotives used on the West Coast. These 3,200-horsepower streamlined diesels are well suited to medium-distance passenger runs where rapid acceleration is desirable. *Brian Solomon*

the 800 series. Later GE refined its design, producing the 4,200-horsepower P42DC built for both Amtrak and Canadian intercity passenger provider VIA Rail. A significantly different dual-mode variety, the P32AC-DM was designed for service on New York–area third-rail DC-electrified lines. Able to operate as both as a diesel-electric and as a straight electric in third-rail territory, this model also employs an alternating current (AC) traction system, rather than the more conventional direct current (DC) traction used on most passenger locomotives.

In the mid-1980s, EMD designed its F59PH model for short-haul passenger services. This wide-nose cab type used EMD's state-of-the-art 710 series engine and modern electrics refined for its 60-series freight diesels. Initially these models were sold to Toronto-based Government of Ontario (GO) Transit, and later to Los Angeles Metrolink.

In the 1990s, EMD adapted the technology used in the F59PH for a new locomotive that complied with California's strict air-quality requirements and had a modern crash-resistant streamlined body featuring the whisper cab. Designated the F59PHI, this 3,200-horsepower model has been ordered for Amtrak corridor services on the West Coast, as well as by the North Carolina Department of Transportation for Amtrak services and by a variety of commuter railroads. EMD also sold specialized 3,000-horsepower models to New York's Long Island Rail Road: One model was a conventional diesel-electric passenger locomotive in a low-clearance body, the other was a very similar-appearing dual-mode type for third-rail service into Penn Station.

Increasingly stringent demands on emissions, combined with new crash-worthiness standards, have made the comparatively small market for passenger locomotives uneconomic to the large locomotive manufacturers. Today, passenger diesels often cost twice that of new freight power. Instead of engineering and building very small fleets of custom-designed passenger locomotives, EMD and GE have acted as suppliers, providing primary components to smaller manufacturers.

MotivePower's MPXpress models have been the most common types purchased by North American commuter railroads in the last decade. Three models have been offered that use EMD-designed engines, trucks, and traction motors in a futuristic-looking locomotive body. In addition, Alstom has built an unusual-looking high-horsepower passenger diesel for New Jersey–based NJ Transit, while Pennsylvania-based Brookville has constructed road switcher–style locomotives for Metro-North and the Connecticut Department of Transportation.

Opposite: One of the United States' newest commuter train services is the *North Star*, which began operations from Minneapolis to far-flung northwestern exurbs in November 2009. The trains serve the downtown Target Field terminal just around the corner from the Voyageur Press offices. The *North Star* operates with five MotivePower MP36PH-3Cs. *Brian Solomon*

In June 2008, a Metrolink F59PHI leads an outbound train at Burbank. The F59PHI was EMD's standard passenger locomotive introduced in the mid-1990s. The model shares styling queues with automotive minivans built by parent company General Motors at about the same time. The model became one of the most common for West Coast services, which expanded rapidly during the 1990s. *Brian Solomon*

On June 30, 2010, Amtrak train No. 42, *The Pennsylvanian,* works east on the former Pennsylvania Railroad main line at Summerhill, Pennsylvania. GE Genesis model P42 No. 44 has the historical significance of having led President Barack Obama's inauguration special on January 17, 2009. Genesis models compose the bulk of Amtrak's intercity diesel locomotive fleet. *Brian Solomon*

New Mexico's Rail Runner suburban service began operations in 2006. Today, its route connects the cities of Santa Fe, Albuquerque, and Belen. By mid-2010, Rail Runner was one of eight North American commuter railways to receive MotivePower's MP36PH-3C diesel-electric locomotives. On St. Patrick's Day 2009, Rail Runner No. 106 passes a former Union Switch & Signal Style-T upper-quadrant semaphore near Bernalillo, New Mexico. *Tim Doherty*

Amtrak General Electric Dash 8-32BWH No. 502 with a *Capitols* train is seen at 16th Street Station in Oakland, California, in 1992. Amtrak's 20 Dash 8-32BWHs built in 1991 were similar to Santa Fe Railway's Dash 8-40BWs freight locomotives and share most external dimensions. However, Amtrak's Dash 8-32BWH is powered by a 12-cylinder FDL engine rated at 3,200 horsepower for traction. An extra alternator is used to produce head-end power for passenger cars—thus the *H* in the locomotive designation. *Brian Solomon*

No. 502 leads a Sacramento-to-San Jose *Capitols* service along the shore of San Pablo Bay near Pinole, California. The new Amtrak livery on these GEs earned the Dash 8-32BWHs the nickname "Pepsi cans." Locomotive Nos. 501 and 502 were funded by the California Department of Transportation, thus indicated by the small blue CT on the nose of the locomotive. *Brian Solomon*

Amtrak's "Pepsi can" scheme was short-lived. On November 12, 2003, Amtrak No. 505, wearing a minimalist Platinum Mist livery, leads a *San Joaquin* train from Bakersfield, California, through Oakland's Jack London Square. Amtrak's order for Dash 8-32BWHs was a prelude to the development of the streamlined Genesis type introduced in 1993. *Brian Solomon*

Amtrak P42DC No. 63, in its as-delivered paint, leads the eastward *Pennsylvanian* near Cresson, Pennsylvania, on the former Pennsylvania Railroad main line. The P42DC was the most common model of General Electric's Genesis. The 4,250-horsepower locomotive began production in 1996 and was sold to both Amtrak and VIA Rail for long-distance passenger services. As built, the P42DC complied with EPA Tier 0 emissions standards. *Brian Solomon*

In October 2000, Amtrak P42DC No. 1, dressed in the Northeast Direct scheme, speeds train No. 449— the westward Boston section of the *Lake Shore Limited*—over the Quaboag River near West Warren, Massachusetts. This Genesis series is no longer produced, in part, because the design complies with neither current EPA emissions standards nor contemporary crashworthiness requirements. *Brian Solomon*

An unusual route for an Amtrak Genesis locomotive is the old Rutland Railroad line via Mount Holly, Vermont. While not part of a regular Amtrak service, on October 4, 2004, a pair of P42DCs leads the *American Orient Express*, a high-priced tour train using 1940s and 1950s streamlined equipment. The train is crossing Vermont Rail System's high trestle at Cuttingsville on its way to Bellows Falls, Vermont. *Brian Solomon*

General Electric's P32AC-DM is a specialized dual-mode (hence "DM") machine that can operate using electricity from New York City–area third rail as well as diesel power. It succeeded EMD's FL9, a type designed in the 1950s for the New Haven Railroad and that worked for many years in New York suburban services. On June 27, 1997, a new Amtrak P32AC-DM leads an Empire Corridor train north in the Hudson Valley toward Albany. *Brian Solomon*

Metro-North operates a fleet of P32AC-DMs on its push-pull suburban services to Grand Central Station. In electrified territory these locomotives can draw current from the line-side third rail, although in routine operations they tend to run as diesels until reaching the Park Avenue Tunnel. On July 9, 2004, at Scarborough, New York, on the former New York Central Hudson Division, No. 227 shoves its train toward New York City. *Brian Solomon*

The Connecticut Department of Transportation purchased four of the P32AC-DMs operated by Metro-North. These are painted in a modern adaptation of New Haven Railroad's famous McGinnis livery best remembered as the scheme used on the dual-mode FL9s. This view of P32AC-DM No. 229 in May 2007 was taken on the former New Haven Railroad at Danbury. *Brian Solomon*

In 2001, Canada's intercity passenger service operator, VIA Rail, acquired a fleet of 20 Genesis P42DCs from General Electric. VIA Rail No. 908 crosses the Lachine Canal in Montreal in October 2004. *Brian Solomon*

VIA Rail typically assigns its Genesis diesels to 1980s-era LRC trains working in the Quebec City–Montreal–Ottawa–Toronto–Windsor corridor. LRC stands for "Light, Rapid, Comfortable" and uses passenger cars with a tilting design built by Bombardier. Originally these trains were hauled by futuristic-looking LRC diesels powered by the Alco-designed 251 engine. *Brian Solomon*

On October 10, 2009, two VIA Rail P42DCs work west at Spadina Avenue after departing Toronto Union Station. *Brian Solomon*

Right: A Chicago Metra F40PHM-2 works west across the diamonds at Joliet, Illinois, on July 30, 1994. This model was unique to the commuter rail operator. Internally, it was very similar to the F40PH-2 and shared its 3,000 horsepower rating; externally, it featured a distinctive cab profile reaching to the front of the locomotive and lacking the distinct nose section featured on F40 models. *Brian Solomon*

Below: EMD developed the F40PH-2 for Amtrak in the mid-1970s and the model remained as a standard new passenger type through the 1980s. In 1990 Metra ordered this variation of the type designated F40PHM-2. Metra's former Burlington commuter route to Aurora serves La Grange, Illinois, pictured here on July 4, 2005. Ironically EMD's La Grange plant ended regular locomotive assembly following completion of the last Metra F40PHM-2 in December 1992. *Brian Solomon*

Opposite: Metra's F40PHM-2s were known colloquially as Winnebagos because of their resemblance to the popular brand of motor home. On June 22, 2004, Metra No. 201 departs Union Station in Chicago with an Aurora-bound suburban train. *Brian Solomon*

Above: Government of Ontario, which operates an intensive suburban service radiating from Toronto Union Station, worked with EMD in the design of a suitable commuter locomotive. A GO Transit F59PH races toward Toronto Union Station on February 8, 2010. Powered by a 12-cylinder 710G3 diesel, the F59PH shares most of its mechanical and electrical equipment with the streamlined F59PHI. *Brian Solomon*

Opposite: For two decades, EMD F59PHs working in push-pull service have provided most of GO Transit's motive power needs. During 2009 and 2010, GO bought new MP40s from MotivePower to supplant the aging F59PHs. *Brian Solomon*

Los Angeles Metrolink developed a commuter rail system for Southern California that was closely modeled on GO Transit's successful strategy. Metrolink bought a small fleet of F59PHs, making it the only other buyer of this relatively unusual model. Between runs, Metrolink No. 860 lays over at Oceanside, California, on May 31, 2008. *Brian Solomon*

Above: EMD adapted its existing F59PH suburban rail-service locomotive into the F59PHI—a powerful, streamlined diesel-electric that complied with strict California emission requirements. On November 4, 2003, F59PHI No. 2012, lettered for Amtrak California, leads a *Capitols* service arriving at San Jose. The F59PHI's bulbous nose is a fiberglass composite; thick steel plates beneath it help protect the crew. This design is safer than the 1940s-era streamlined "bulldog" nose used on EMD E- and F-units. Brian *Solomon*

Opposite top: Amtrak F59PHI No. 450 works at the back of a *Pacific Surfliner* passing Del Mar, California. While General Electric's Genesis models have become standard for most Amtrak long-distance services, EMD's F59PHI is the most common type on various West Coast corridor trains. *Brian Solomon*

Opposite bottom: The modern-looking F59PHI was styled to match specially designed bi-level low-entry "California cars." On September 15, 2009, Amtrak No. 2008 crosses wetlands at Alviso, California, with a *Capitols* train. *Brian Solomon*

The North Carolina DOT bought two F59PHIs in 1998 for use on the *Piedmont*. *City of Salisbury* and *City of Asheville* carry road numbers that represent the founding dates of those cities and represent an operational anomaly: The majority of F59PHIs in the United States are assigned to West Coast passenger services. *Brian Solomon*

Amtrak's Raleigh-to-Charlotte *Piedmont* approaches its station stop at Durham, North Carolina, on February 19, 2004. This three-car train is hauled by F59PHI No. 1755, *City of Salisbury*. The North Carolina Department of Transportation funds the train and, because of lower long-term operating costs, made the unusual choice of buying new EMD locomotives to haul refurbished heritage passenger equipment. *Brian Solomon*

Montreal commuter train operator Agence métropolitaine de transport (AMT) operates 11 EMD F59PHIs (Nos. 1320–1330) built in 2000 and 2001. On August 16, 2004, No. 1325 is seen at Vendome Station across from a rebuilt GP9, classed GP9RM. AMT's F59PHIs primarily work the CP Rail route between Montreal and Vaudreuil-Hudson, Quebec (a commuter route that formerly ended at Dorion). *Tim Doherty*

Above: Long Island Rail Road's EMD DM30AC was designed specifically for New York–area suburban service. It features 45-inch wheels and a 92:19 gear ratio with Siemens-designed AC traction motors capable of 100-mile-per-hour service. *Brian Solomon*

Opposite bottom: LIRR's dual-mode DM30AC No. 500 leads a train of bi-level Kawasaki cars on the Central Branch at Bethpage, New York, on April 20, 2000. LIRR operates one of the most intensive commuter rail networks in the United States. These modern EMD passenger locomotives are unique to LIRR and are custom-designed with a low profile to accommodate tight clearances in the New York City area. *Patrick Yough*

On March 12, 2003, LIRR DM30AC No. 510 approaches Jamaica, Queens, with a double-deck suburban train. LIRR's 23 DM30ACs (sometimes classified as DE30AC-DMs) are modern dual-mode locomotives rated at 3,000-horsepower. They can operate as normal diesel-electric locomotives or draw current from a high-voltage DC third rail. Numbered in the 500 series, they are similar in appearance to LIRR's 23 400 series DE30ACs, which are diesel-electric only. *Brian Solomon*

Above: Brookville's BL20GH rides on Blomberg trucks powered by D78 traction motors. On July 20, 2010, a Connecticut Department of Transportation Brookville-built BL20GH leads an afternoon train from Waterbury along the electrified former New Haven Railroad main line.
Patrick Yough

Opposite top: On June 9, 2008—its first day of public operation—CDOT Brookville-built BL20GH No. 125 leads train No. 1906 at Waterbury. CDOT bought six of these unusual locomotives, primarily to replace its aging FL9s and FP10s on branch passenger trains.
Otto M. Vondrak

Opposite bottom: Dressed in a livery inspired by the New Haven Railroad's famous McGinnis paint scheme, BL20GH No. 125 leads train No. 1841 at Stamford on July 6, 2009.
Otto M. Vondrak

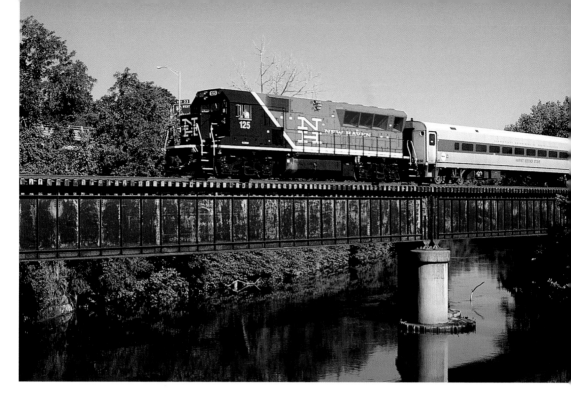

In 2003, Caltrain Peninsula service, which operates the former Southern Pacific commutes between San Francisco and San Jose (and a few trains to Gilroy), was the first to acquire MotivePower's MPXpress commuter locomotives. These were bought for service expansion and improvement in the form of the "Baby Bullet" limited express trains designed to cut running time between main terminals and provide additional services at rush hours. The locomotives arrived prior to introduction of Baby Bullet services and initially worked ordinary Caltrain runs. *Brian Solomon*

Caltrain MP36PH-3C No. 927 departs Millbrae Station on August 13, 2009, with a San Jose–bound Baby Bullet. These 3,600-horsepower locomotives have 20 percent more horsepower than Caltrain's 1980s-era EMD F40PH-2s. *Brian Solomon*

A San Francisco–bound Baby Bullet roars past California Avenue Station in Palo Alto. Today these powerful diesels roar over the line once famous for Southern Pacific's *Daylight* streamliners. *Brian Solomon*

An MP36PH-3S and an F40PHM-2 work a westward "scoot" running from Chicago Union Station to Aurora, Illinois, on the old Burlington route. As of late 2010, Chicago Metra has been the only operator of the MP36PH-3S variation of MotivePower's MPXpress passenger locomotive. The MP36PH-3S uses a static inverter driven by the prime mover for head-end power (HEP). The MP36PH-3C model produces HEP with an auxiliary diesel and separate generator. *Brian Solomon*

Metra MP36PH-3S No. 424 shoves at the back of a suburban train working toward Chicago Union Station on June 22, 2004. *Brian Solomon*

MotivePower MP40PH-3Cs have replaced 1980s-era EMD F59PHs as the standard locomotive on most GO Transit trains. All trains are push-pull sets with the locomotive on the east end. On June 11, 2010, GO Transit No. 631 shoves a westward train at Bathurst Street in Toronto. *Brian Solomon*

Toronto offers one of the best integrated public transportation networks in North America. Using GO Transit and Toronto Transit Commission subways, streetcars, and buses, it is easy to travel virtually anywhere in the metropolitan area without a car. *Brian Solomon*

Freezing conditions prevailed on February 8, 2010, as a GO Transit MP40PH-3C worked eastward with a train inbound for Toronto Union Station. Among GO Transit's unusual features is that many trains work through Union Station to outlying suburban terminals rather than terminating downtown. *Brian Solomon*

Switchers

istorically, switchers were among the most common types of diesel locomotives; however, from the 1960s through the 1980s, their market declined rapidly. Due to the nature of their service, switchers tend to have longer lifespans than road power and therefore require less frequent replacement. Also, many railroads cascaded old road diesels into switching duties rather than buy new switchers. Finally, a shift from small carload shipments to point-to-point intermodal and single-commodity unit trains, as well as a general decline in passenger services and moves to fixed passenger consists, further obviated the need for switchers.

In the 1990s, the market for new switchers heated up again. Modern high-horsepower road locomotives, which tend to be equipped with North American Safety Cabs, are poorly suited for most switching duties. Also, innovative technologies have made modern switching locomotives more economical to operate than traditional models. However, because demand for switchers is still relatively small, this market doesn't interest General Electric and EMD, so smaller manufacturers have developed the modern

switcher business, building all-new switchers, as well as rebuilding, remanufacturing, or otherwise adapting older types with state-of-the-art equipment.

In the early 1990s, MK Rail (antecedent to today's MotivePower Industries) developed an experimental low-horsepower, low-emissions switcher that burned liquefied natural gas. While LNG-fueled locomotives did not catch on, during the last decade, development and application of Genset (a compact engine-generator set) technology has been one of the most successful means of reducing fuel consumption and lowering emissions for new switching locomotives. Low-emissions diesel Gensets are used in multiple in place of conventional single large diesel engines. Where a large engine must run all the time, individual Gensets are switched on only as needed, resulting in more efficient fuel consumption and much lower emissions. Computer controls may rotate the use of Gensets to ensure relatively even wear and maintenance.

Several railroads have entered public-private partnerships in which public agencies provide funding assistance for railroads to replace traditional diesels with new Genset locomotives. California and Texas, where emissions requirements are the most stringent, have led the nation in Genset locomotive applications.

In 2010, several manufacturers offered Genset locomotives, including National Railway Equipment, Railpower, Brookville, and MotivePower. NRE offers four Genset locomotive models in its N-ViroMotive line, including three four-axle, four-motor types: the 1GS-7B is a single-Genset locomotive rated at 700 horsepower; the 2GS-14B is a twin-Genset 1,400-horsepower model; and the 3GS-21B is a 2,100-horsepower triple-Genset aimed at replacing the 2,000 GP38s and GP38-2s in equivalent services. NRE's 3GS-21C, a triple-Genset six-motor model also rated at 2,100 horsepower, is roughly equivalent to an EMD SD38 and is intended for slow-speed, high tractive–effort applications, such as hump yard service. Most NRE locomotives use Cummins QSK19C diesels

Railpower, owned by short-line operator R. J. Corman since 2009, has enjoyed reasonable success with its range of Genset locomotives. These include two four-axle, four-motor models and one six-motor type.

The RP14BD is a twin-Genset type built on an old switcher platform and rated at 1,400 horsepower, while the RP20BD is a triple-Genset built on an old EMD GP9-era platform and rated at 2,000 horsepower. The six-motor RP20CD is built on an old EMD platform and rated at 2,000 horsepower. Typically, Railpower locomotives have employed Deutz V-8 diesels, although company literature notes that Cummins diesels are also available.

Union Pacific has been a leader in Genset locomotive development and application, and it has several fleets in dedicated service. As of August 2010, it rostered 175 units: a fleet of 60 NRE 2GS-21Bs (UP class 2GS-21B) and a lone 2GS-14B are assigned to California's Los Angeles Basin, while another fleet of 98 Railpower four-motor RP20Bs were based in Texas working largely around Ft. Worth and Houston. UP's smallest fleet consists of six-axle Railpower RP20CDs that work the former Southern Pacific yard at Roseville, California. BNSF also has a significant fleet of NRE and Railpower Gensets, largely assigned to terminals in California and Texas.

Previous pages:
Railpower RP20BD No. 5400 is a 2,000-horsepower switcher powered by three Deutz diesel Gensets (compact diesel-generator units). Although these modern switchers are commonly referred to as Gensets, the term properly applies to the powerplants within the locomotive, rather than the locomotive itself. *Pat Yough*

Because of ther low emissions, three-Genset, six-motor switching locomotives tend to be assigned in areas where pollution control has popular political considerations. *Brian Solomon*

Union Pacific No. 2690 is a Railpower three-Genset, four-motor RP20BD (also variously referred to as a RP20B and RP30GE) assigned to switching work in Texas. *Pat Yough*

UP has assigned six Railpower three-Genset, six-motor locomotives to the Roseville, California, hump yard. These are powered by Deutz diesels and designed for slow-speed high-tractive effort service. In May 2008, UP displayed one of the brand-new Genset locomotives at the California State Railroad Museum in Sacramento. *Brian Solomon*

Above: National Railway Equipment's four stock varieties of its N-ViroMotive Genset switchers were developed between 2001 and 2005 to meet strict air-quality regulations imposed by the California Air Quality Resources Board. BNSF 3GS-21B No. 1253, seen at Mykawa, Texas, on June 6, 2009, is a four-motor unit riding on Blomberg trucks with a 62:18 gear ratio and D77 traction motors. Its three 700-horsepower Gensets each use a Cummins QSK19 paired with a 572RDL generator. *Tom Kline*

Opposite top: California's Pacific Harbor Line acquired four National Railway Equipment four-motor 3GS-12B Genset locomotives during 2007 and 2008, and it also owns a pair of NRE's six-motor 3GS-12C Genset locomotives. The "B" and "C" designations denote four or six motors, as all axles are powered. Pacific Harbor Line provides switching at the ports of Los Angeles and Long Beach. *Brian Solomon*

Opposite bottom: BNSF switches at Point Richmond, California, with National Railway Equipment 3GS-12B Genset locomotive No. 1286 on May 29, 2010. *Philip A. Brahms*

A Buffalo & Pittsburgh crewman works Genesee & Wyoming locomotive No. 1401, a Brookville GS1400. This 1,400-horsepower locomotive features a pair of diesel Gensets, each using a Cummins QSK19 engine. The locomotive frame and some mechanical components have been recycled from an older EMD SW1500 switcher. Railroads can lower the emissions and improve the fuel economy of switching locomotives by replacing traditional large diesel engines with groups of two or more diesel Gensets because two (or more) Gensets are active only when the load on the locomotive requires greater power.
Patrick Yough

Brand-new G&W No. 1401 lettered for Buffalo & Pittsburgh works at Butler Yard near Punxsutawney, Pennsylvania, on July 17, 2010. G&W's Buffalo & Pittsburgh operates former Buffalo, Rochester & Pittsburgh trackage in western Pennsylvania and New York State acquired from CSX in 1988 as part of a regional spin-off. *Adam Stuebgen*

183

Two Port Terminal Railway Association MK1500Ds work a chemical train at Penn City Yard in Channelview, east of Houston, Texas, on June 12, 2004. MK Rail built 24 MK1500Ds in 1996 for the PTRA. These are the road's sole motive power for switching service in the Houston area. No. 9617 began its career as New York Central GP7 No. 5610 in the early 1950s. *Tom Kline*

BNSF MK1200G No. 1203 rests at San Pedro, California. Introduced in 1994 by MotivePower Industries predecessor MK Rail, this was an experimental low-emissions design powered by a Caterpillar G3516 engine and fueled by liquefied natural gas. Two were built for Santa Fe and two for Union Pacific. Today, BNSF rosters all four, which are usually assigned switching work in the Los Angeles area. *Brian Solomon*

This MK1500D was built at Boise, Idaho, in November 1996. After separating from MK Rail in 1996, MotivePower Industries was known as Boise Locomotive Company for three years until it merged with Westinghouse Air Brake Company. Today, MotivePower continues to build a variety of specialty locomotives. *Patrick Yough*

MotivePower built 13 MP20GPs for Union Pacific using old GP50 platforms. These are assigned to switching work in the Houston area. UP has numbered its switchers and other locomotives in yard work with UPY reporting marks. UPY No. 2109 was photographed at Houston, Texas, on April 1, 2007. *Tom Kline*

As traditional switchers wear out, the Class 1 railroads have had to replace them with new, rebuilt, or otherwise improved machines. *Tom Kline*

A detail view of a Union Pacific MP20GP control stand. *Tom Kline*

Books

Armstrong, John H. *The Railroad: What It Is, What It Does*. Omaha, Neb.: Simmons-Boardman Books, 1982.

Bush, Donald J. *The Streamlined Decade*. New York: Braziller, 1975.

Churella, Albert, J. *From Steam to Diesel*. Princeton, N.J.: Princeton University Press, 1998.

Diesel Era. The Revolutionary Diesel: EMC's FT. Halifax, Pa.: Withers Publishing, 1994.

Garmany, John B. *Southern Pacific Dieselization*. Edmonds, Wash.: Pacific Fast Mail, 1985.

Jennison, Brian, and Victor Neves. *Southern Pacific Oregon Division*. Mukilteo, Wash.: Hundman Publishing, 1997.

Kirkland, John, F. *The Diesel Builders Vols. I, II, & III*. Glendale, Calif.: Interurban Press, 1983.

————. *Dawn of the Diesel Age*. Pasadena, Calif.: Interurban Press, 1994.

Lloyd, Gordon Jr., and Louis A. Marre. *Conrail Motive Power Review, Vol. 1*. Glendale, Calif.: Interurban Press, 1992.

Marre, Louis A. *Diesel Locomotives: The First 50 Years*. Waukesha, Wis.: Kalmbach Publishing Company, 1995.

Marre, Louis A., and Jerry A. Pinkepank. *The Contemporary Diesel Spotter's Guide*. Milwaukee, Wis.: Kalmbach Publishing, 1985.

Marre, Louis A., and Paul K. Withers. *The Contemporary Diesel Spotter's Guide, Year 2000 Ed*. Halifax, Pa.: Withers Publishing, 2000.

McDonald, Charles W. *Diesel Locomotive Rosters*. Milwaukee, Wis.: Kalmbach Publishing, 1982.

McDonnell, Greg. *U-Boats: General Electric Diesel Locomotives*. Toronto: Boston Mills Press, 1994.

Pinkepank, Jerry A. *The Diesel Spotter's Guide*. Milwaukee, Wis.: Kalmbach Publishing, 1967.

————. *The Second Diesel Spotter's Guide*. Milwaukee, Wis.: Kalmbach Publishing, 1973.

Reck, Franklin M. *On Time*. LaGrange, Ill.: Electro-Motive Division of General Motors, 1948.

Saunders, Richard Jr. *Merging Lines: American Railroads 1900–1970*. DeKalb, Ill.: Northern Illinois University Press, 2001.

Solomon, Brian. *Southern Pacific Railroad*. Osceola, Wis.: MBI Publishing Company, 1999.

————. *The American Diesel Locomotive*. Osceola, Wis.: MBI Publishing Company, 2000.

————. *Locomotive*. St. Paul, Minn.: MBI Publishing Company, 2001.

————. *Burlington Northern Santa Fe Railway*. St. Paul, Minn.: MBI Publishing Company, 2005.

————. *CSX*. St. Paul, Minn.: MBI Publishing Company, 2005.

Staff, Virgil. *D-Day on the Western Pacific*. Glendale, Calif.: Interurban Press, 1982.

Strack, Don. *Union Pacific 2000: Locomotive Directory*. Halifax, Pa.: Withers Publishing, 2000.

Strapac, Joseph A. *Southern Pacific Review 1952–1982*. Huntington Beach, Calif.: Pacific Coast Chapter of the Railway and Locomotive Historical Society, 1983.

————. *Southern Pacific Review 1953–1985*. Huntington Beach, Calif.: Pacific Coast Chapter of the Railway and Locomotive Historical Society, 1986.

————. *Southern Pacific Historic Diesels Vol 3–10*. Huntington Beach, Calif., and Bellflower, Calif.: Shade Tree Books, 2003.

Westing, Frederick. *Erie Power*. Medina, Ohio: Alvin F. Staufer, 1970.

Withers, Paul K. *Conrail Motive Power Review 1986–1991*. Halifax, Pa.: Withers Publishing, 1992.

————. *Norfolk Southern Locomotive Directory 2001*. Halifax, Pa: Withers Publishing, 2001.

Periodicals

CTC Board: Railroads Illustrated, Ferndale, Wash.

Diesel Era, Halifax, Pa.

Extra 2200 South, Cincinnati, Ohio.

Jane's World Railways, London.

Official Guide to the Railways, New York.

Passenger Train Journal, Waukesha, Wis. [no longer published]

Passenger Train Annual, Nos. 3 & 4, Park Forest, Ill. [no longer published]

RailNews. Waukesha, Wis. [no longer published]

Railroad History, formerly *Railway and Locomotive Historical Society Bulletin*. Boston, Mass.

Railway Age, Chicago and New York.

Shoreliner, Grafton, Mass.

Southern Pacific Bulletin, San Francisco.

The Railway Gazette, London.

Trains. Waukesha, Wis.

Vintage Rails. Waukesha, Wis. [no longer published]

Manuals, Timetables, and Brochures

Amtrak. *Operating Instructions F40PH/P30CH Diesel-Electric Locomotives*. 1986.

General Electric. *New Series Diesel-Electric Locomotive Operating Manual*. Erie, Pa., 1979.

————. *Series-7 Diesel-Electric Locomotives*. Erie, Pa., 1980.

————. *Achieving a Leadership Position in Turbocharger Technology*. Erie, Pa., 1982.

————. *A New Generation for Increased Productivity*. Erie, Pa., 1984.

————. *A New Generation for Increased Productivity*. Erie, Pa., 1987.

————. *GE Diesel Engines: Power for Progress*. Erie, Pa., 1988.

————. *GENESIS Series*. Erie, Pa., 1993.

——————. *GENESIS Series 2 P32AC-DM Operating Manual.* Erie, Pa., 1998.

Electro-Motive Division. *GP40X Operator's Manual.* La Grange, Ill., 1977.

——————. *SD45 Operator's Manual.* La Grange, Ill., 1977.

——————. *F40PH Operator's Manual.* La Grange, Ill., 1978.

——————. *F40PH-2C Operator's Manual.* La Grange, Ill., 1988.

——————. *SD70M Operator's Manual.* La Grange, Ill., 1994.

——————. *SD80MAC Locomotive Operation Manual.* La Grange, Ill., 1996.

Seaboard Coast Line. *Instructions and Information Pertaining to Diesel Electric Engines.* Jacksonville, Fla., 1972.

Websites

www.brookvilleequipment.com

www.emdiesels.com/emdweb/products/loco_index.jsp

www.getransportation.com

www.motivepower-wabtec.com/locomotives/commuter/mpxpress.php

www.nationalrailway.com

www.rjcorman.com/railpower.html

www.transport.alstom.com